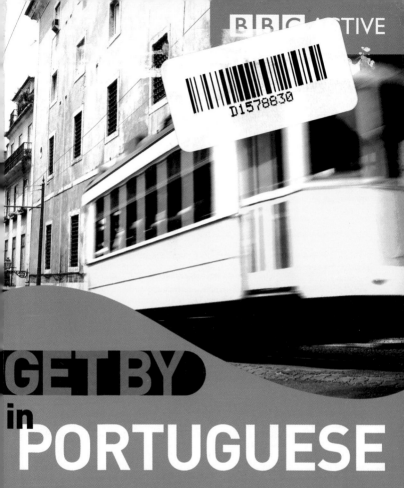

BBC ACTIVE

GET BY
in
PORTUGUESE

PETER BULL
MATTHEW HANCOCK

LANGUAGE CONSULTANT:
...ELLYN

BBC Active, an imprint of Educational Publishers LLP, part of the Pearson Education Group
Edinburgh Gate, Harlow, Essex CM20 2JE, England

© Educational Publishers LLP 2007

BBC logo © BBC 1996. BBC and BBC ACTIVE are trademarks of the British Broadcasting
Corporation

First edition published 1998. This edition published 2007.

ISBN-13: 978-1-4066-1272-1

Cover design: Emma Wallace
Cover photograph: George Doyle/Getty Images
Insides concept design: Nicolle Thomas
Layout: Rob Lian
Commissioning editor: Debbie Marshall
Project editor: Melanie Kramers
Project assistant: Hannah Beatson
Senior production controller: Man Fai Lau
Marketing: Fiona Griffiths, Paul East

Printed in China. (CTPS/01)
The Publisher's policy is to use paper manufactured from sustainable forests.

All photographs supplied by Alamy Images.
p9 Peter Horree; p10 Didi; p12 Martyn Vickery; p15 isifa Image Service s.r.o.; p16
mediacolor's; p24 Robert Harding Picture Library Ltd; p27 Ken Welsh; p31 Oliver
Gerhard; p32 Cristian Baitg Schreiweis; p34 Purple Marbles; p40 blickwinkel; p42 Cro
Magnon; p44 Andrew Linscott; p45 Cro Magnon; p48 Danita Delimont; p55 eye35.com;
p58 Simon Reddy; p60 JLImages; p62 Eddie Gerald; p63 Sébastien Baussais; p65 Ernst
Wrba; p72 Alan Copson City Pictures; p74 Dbimages; p76 Yadid Levy; p82 eye35; p85
Ken Welsh; p87 CuboImages srl; p89 Yadid Levy; p94 Cro Magnon; p98 Stockfolio; p100
Michael Howard; p103 Popperfoto; p104 World Pictures; p108 Michael Howard; p109
George Brewin; p114 Photolocate; p116 Andy Arthur; p122 Colin Walton

Contents

Get By in Portuguese is divided into colour-coded topics to help you find what you need quickly. Each unit contains practical travel tips to help you get around and understand the country, and a phrasemaker, to help you say what you need to and understand what you hear.

As well as listing key phrases, **Get By in Portuguese** aims to help you understand how the language works so that you can build your own phrases and start to communicate independently. The check out dialogues show the language in action, and the try it out activities give you an opportunity to practise for yourself. The link up sections pick out the key structures and give helpful notes about their use. A round-up of basic grammar can be found in the Language Builder, pp129-136.

In Portuguese, all nouns (things, people, concepts) are either masculine or feminine and this affects the way they are written and pronounced as well as the words related to them. In the book these alternative endings are shown: masculine/feminine e.g. amigo/a, meaning male friend/female friend.

If you've bought the pack with the audio CD, you'll be able to listen to a selection of the most important phrases and check out dialogues, as well as all the as if you were there activities. You can use the book on its own – but the CD will help you to improve your pronunciation.

sounds Portuguese

To help you start speaking Portuguese, this book uses a pronunciation guide, based on sounds you already know. This is only an approximation of the Portuguese sounds – the best way to improve pronunciation is by listening to native speakers. Key points to remember are also highlighted in the sound checks throughout the units. Note that, although Portugal is next to Spain and many words look like Spanish, there is a big difference in pronunciation.

nasal sounds

An important new sound is 'nasalisation': when you pronounce a vowel sound through your mouth and nose at the same time. Nasal sounds are present in words with a til (~) over the stressed vowel.

pão *pãhoo*   pensão *pehnsãhoo*   cartões *kahrtoheensh*

Or before or after an m or n:

sem *saheem*   tem *taheem*   tinto *teeñtoo*

stress

When a word has a written accent, always put the stress on that part of the word. Stress is shown in this book in bold italics.

café *kah**fe***　　　　　　　　táxi ***tak**see*　　　　　　　água *a**goo**ah*

When there is no accent and the word ends in a vowel, stress the last but one syllable:

queria *ku**ree**ah*　　　　　　　casado *kah**za**doo*

When there is no accent and the word ends in a consonant, stress the last syllable:

comprar *kohm**prar***　　　　　　jornal *joor**nal***

Exceptions are words ending in -m or -s:

mensagem *mehn**sa**jaheem*　　　minutos *mee**noo**toosh*

vowels

Stressed vowels are consistent and clear but unstressed vowels have a very soft sound and in some cases almost disappear.

		sounds like ...	shown as ...
a	(stressed)	'a' in 'cat'	*a*
	(unstressed)	'a' in 'across'	*ah*
e	(stressed)	'e' in 'belt' or	*e*
		'e' in 'empty'	*eh*
	(stressed)	'u' in 'uncle'	*u*
		hardly pronounced at the end	
i		'ee' in 'leek'	*ee*
o	(stressed)	'o' in 'pot'	*o*
		'au' in 'caught'	*oh*
	(unstressed)	'oo' in 'cook'	*oo*
		hardly pronounced at the end	
u		'oo' in 'cook'	*oo*

consonants

Most Portuguese consonants are pronounced in much the same way as in English. Exceptions are listed on the next page:

		sounds like ...	shown as ...
c	+ **e** or **i**	's' in 'sit'	s
c	+ all other vowels	'k' in 'kit'	k
ç		's' in 'sit'	s
ch		'sh' in 'she'	sh
g	+ **e** or **i**	's' in 'pleasure'	j
	+ all other vowels	'g' in 'good'	g
		'sh' in 'she'	j
h	NOT pronounced		h
lh	in middle of word/ between vowels	'lli' in 'million'	ll
nh		'ni' in 'onion'	ny
r	between vowels or at end of word	'r' in 'rock'	r
			r
	at beginning of word, and double (rr)	like Scottish 'r', rolled strongly	rr
			rr
s	at beginning of word	's' in 'sit'	s
	between vowels	'z' in 'zip'	z
	at end/middle of word or before consonant	'sh' in 'she'	sh
ss		's' in 'sit'	s
x	at beginning of word	'sh' in 'she'	sh
	at middle of word	'z' in 'zip' or 's' in 'sit'	z or s
		'x' in 'six'	ks
z	at beginning/middle of word	'z' in 'zip'	z
	at end of word	'sh' in 'she'	sh

pronouncing the alphabet

A *a*	**B** *beh*	**C** *seh*	**D** *deh*	**E** *e*
F *ef*	**G** *geh*	**H** *ahga*	**I** *ee*	**J** *jotah*
K *ka*pah	**L** *el*	**M** *em*	**N** *en*	**O** *o*
P *peh*	**Q** *keh*	**R** *err*	**S** *es*	**T** *teh*
U *oo*	**V** *veh*	**W** *double u* (veh-**doo**ploo)	**X** *sheesh*	**Y** *eep-seelon*
Z *zeh*				

Bare **Necessities**

phrasemaker

greetings
you may say …

Hello!	Olá!	*ola*
Good morning.	Bom dia.	*bohm̃ **dee**ah*
Good afternoon.	Boa tarde.	***boh**ah **tard***
Good evening/night.	Boa noite.	***boh**ah **nohee**t*
How do you do?	Muito prazer.	*moo**eeñ**too prah**zehr***
Nice to meet you.	Muito prazer em …	*moo**eeñ**too prah**zehr** a**heem̃***
(to a man)	conhecê-lo.	*koonnyeh**seh**loo*
(to a woman)	conhecê-la.	*koonnyeh**seh**lah*
How are you?	Como está?	***koh**moo eesh**ta***
Fine, and you?	Bem, e …	*ba**heem̃**ee*
(formal, to a man)	o senhor?	*oo sunn**yohr***
(formal, to a woman)	a senhora?	*ah sunn**yoh**rah*
(informal)	você?	*vo**sêh***
very well	muito bem	*moo**eeñ**too ba**heem̃***
See you later.	Até logo.	*ah**te lo**goo*
See you tomorrow.	Até amanhã.	*ah**te** amah**ñnyāh***
Goodbye.	Adeus.	*ah**deh**oosh*

other useful words
you may say …

Excuse me! (to attract attention)	Desculpe!	*dush**koolp***
Excuse me. (to get by in a crowd)	Com licença.	*kohm̃ lee**sehñ**sah*

yes/no	sim/não	*seem̃/nãhoo*
please	por favor/se faz favor	*poor fah**vohr**/su fash fah**vohr***
thank you (very much)	(muito) obrigado/ obrigada	***mooee**ñto obree**ga**doo/ obree**ga**dah*
sorry	desculpe	*dush**kool**p*
It doesn't matter./ It's all right.	Tanto faz./Não faz mal.	*tah**ñ**too fash/nãhoo fash mal*
You're welcome.	Não tem de quê.	*nãhoo taheem̃ du keh*

is/are there ...?

you may say ...

Is there a lift?	Há elevador?	*a eeluvah**dohr***
Are there any toilets?	Há casas de banho?	*a ka**zahsh du bah**ñnyoo*

check out 1

You meet a neighbour on the way to the shops.

○ Olá!
  *o**la***

- Olá! Como está?
  *o**la**. **koh**moo eesh**ta***

○ Bem, e você?
  *ba**heem̃** ee vo**seh***

- Muito bem, obrigado. Até amanhã!
  mooee**ñtoo ba**heem̃** obree**ga**doo. ah**te** amahñ**nyãh

○ Adeus!
  *ah**deh**oosh*

When do you expect to see your neighbour again?

CASTELO

where is/are ...?

you may say ...

Where is ... the town centre?	Onde é ... o centro da cidade?	*ohnd e* *oo sehñtroo dah* *seedadu*
Where are ... the fitting rooms?	Onde são ... os provadores?	*ohnd sãhoo* *oosh* *proovahdohrush*

you may hear ...

É ... à direita à esquerda.	*e* *a deeraheetah* *a eeshkehrdah*	It's ... on the right on the left.	
São ... (sempre) em frente.	*sãhoo* *(sehmpru) aheeñ* *frehnt*	They're ... straight on.	
no fim.	*noo feeñ*	at the end.	

do you have any ...?

you may say ...

Do you have any ... unleaded petrol?	Tem ... gasolina sem chumbo?	*taheeñ* *gahzooleenah* *saheeñ shoomboo*
prawns?	gambas?	*gahñbahsh*

how much ...?

you may say ...

How much does it/ do they cost?	Quanto custa/ custam?	*kwahñtoo kooshtah/* *kooshtahñ*
How much is that (altogether)?	Quanto é (tudo) isso?	*kwahñtoo e (toodoo)* *eesoo*
How much are ... per kilo? the onions the tomatoes	Quanto custam ... por quilo? as cebolas os tomates	*kwahñtoo kooshtahñ* *... poor keeloo* *ahsh subohlahsh* *oosh toomatush*

I'd like …

you may say …

| I'd like …
 a shirt.
 a melon. | Queria …
 uma camisa.
 um melão. | *kureeah*
 oomah kahmeezah
 oom mulãhoo |
| I'd like a kilo of oranges. | Queria um quilo de laranjas. | *kureeah oom keeloo*
 du lahrahñjahsh |

getting things straight

you may say …

Pardon?	Como disse?	*kohmoo deesu*
Could you say that again?	Pode repetir isso?	*pod ruputeer eesoo*
I don't understand.	Não compreendo.	*nãhoo* *kohmpreeehndoo*
More slowly, please.	Mais devagar, se faz favor.	*maeesh duvahgar su* *fash fahvohr*
What does it mean?	O que quer dizer?	*oo ku ker dizehr*
I don't know.	Não sei.	*nãhoo sahee*

about yourself

you may say ...

My name is ...	Chamo-me ...	*shah*moomu
I'm ... (m/f name)	Sou o/a ...	*soh oo/ah*
I'm from ...	Sou de ...	*soh du*
I'm a nurse.	Sou enfermeiro/a.	*soh ehnfur**mahee**roo/ah*
I'm Irish. (See nationalities, p17)	Sou irlandês/ irlandesa.	*soh eerlahnd**êhsh**/ eerlahnd**êzah***
I speak a little Portuguese.	Falo um pouco de português.	*faloo oom* **poh**koo du poortoo**gêhsh**
I'm here on ... holiday. business.	Estou aqui ... de férias. em negócios.	*eeshtoh ah**kee*** *du* **fe**reeahsh *aheem neh**go**seeoosh*
I'm in Portugal for ... two days. one week.	Estou em Portugal por ... dois dias. uma semana.	*eeshtoh aheem poortoogal poor* *doheesh* **dee**ahsh **oo**mah su**mah**nah
I live in ...	Moro em ...	**mo**roo aheem
I work in ...	Trabalho em ...	trah**ba**lloo aheem
I'm ... married. single. a widower/widow.	Sou ... casado/a. solteiro/a. viúvo/viúva.	*soh* kah**za**doo/ah sol**tahee**roo/ah vee**oo**voo/ah
I have ... two children. a boy and a girl.	Tenho ... dois filhos. um rapaz e uma rapariga.	*tah**ñ**nyoo* *doheesh* **fee**lloosh *oom* rrah**pash** *ee* **oo**mah rrahpah**ree**gah
I'm ... years old.	Tenho ... anos.	*tah**ñ**nyoo ... ah*noosh

you may hear ...

Qual é o seu nome?	*kwal e oo **seh**oo nohm*	What's your name?
Donde é?	*dohnd e*	Where are you from?
Tem filhos?	*taheem **fee**llossh*	Do you have children?
Que idade tem?	*keh ee**da**du taheem*	How old are you?

check out 2

You get chatting to a fellow guest in your hotel.

○ Boa tarde. Chamo-me Paula.
*boh*ah tard. *shah*moomu paula

- Chamo-me Andrew.
*shah*moomu andrew

○ Muito prazer.
*mooee*ñtoo prah*zehr*

- Sou de Lagos.
soh du lagosh

○ Eu sou de Newport. Estou aqui em negócios. E você?
*ehoo soh du newport. eesh*toh *ah*kee *aheeñ nugo*seeoosh.
e vo*seh*

- Sou professora de inglês em Lisboa.
*soh proofu*soh*rah du eenglêhsh aheeñ leesh*boh*ah*

○ Mora em Lisboa?
*mo*rah aheeñ leesh*boh*ah

- Sim, moro no centro da cidade.
*seeñ mo*roo noo *sehñ*troo dah see*dad*

Q Is it morning or afternoon?
You're in Portugal on holiday: true or false?

changing money

you may say ...

What's the exchange rate (for the pound)?	Qual é o câmbio (da libra)?	*kwal e oo kahm̃beeoo (dah leebrah)*
I want to change ... £20/$20.	Queria trocar ... vinte libras/dólares.	*kureea trookar veent leebrahsh/dolahrush*
Can I get money out on my credit card?	Posso levantar dinheiro com o meu cartão de crédito?	*posoo luvahntar deenyaheeroo kohm̃ oo mehoo kahrtãhoo du kredeetoo*
one pound (sterling)	uma libra esterlina	*oomah leebrah eeshturleenah*

you may hear ...

Posso ver o seu passaporte?	*posoo vehr oo sehoo pasahport*	May I see your passport?
A comissão que cobramos é ...	*ah koomeesãhoo ku koobrahmoosh e*	The commission charge is ...
dois (euros) cinquenta (cêntimos)	*doheesh (eroosh) seeñkwehñtah (sehnteemoosh)*	€2.50

the time

you may say ...

What time is it?	Que horas são?	*ku orahsh sãhoo*
What time do you ... open? close?	A que horas ... abre? fecha?	*ah ku orahsh abru fehshah*
What time does it ... leave? arrive?	A que horas ... parte? chega?	*ah ku orahsh part shehgah*
What time does it ...? start? finish?	A que horas ... começa? acaba?	*ah ku orahsh koomesah ahkabah*

13

you may hear ...

É uma hora.	*e **oo**mah **o**rah*	It's one o'clock.
São duas horas.	*sãhoo **doo**ahsh **o**rahsh*	It's two o'clock.
São duas e dez.	*sãhoo **doo**ahsh ee desh*	It's ten past two.
São duas e um quarto.	*sãhoo **doo**ahsh ee oõm**kwar**too*	It's quarter past two.
São duas e meia.	*sãhoo **doo**ahsh ee **mahee**ah*	It's half past two.
São vinte para as três.	*sãhoo veent **pah**rah ahsh trehsh*	It's twenty to three.
É um quarto para as cinco.	*e oõm **kwar**too **pah**rah ahsh **seeñ**koo*	It's a quarter to five.
treze (horas) e vinte (minutos)	*trêhz **o**rahsh ee veent mee**noo**toosh*	13.20
à uma hora	*a **oo**mah **o**rah*	at one o'clock
às duas horas	*ash **doo**ahsh **o**rahsh*	at two o'clock

numbers

0	zero	*ze*roo	14	catorze	*kah**tohr**z*
1	um, uma	*oõm/ **oo**mah*	15	quinze	*keeñz*
			16	dezasseis	*duzah- **saheesh***
2	dois, duas	*doheesh/ **doo**ahsh*	17	dezassete	*duzah**set***
3	três	*trehsh*	18	dezoito	*duza- **hohee**too*
4	quatro	***kwa**troo*	19	dezanove	*duzah**nov***
5	cinco	***seeñ**koo*	20	vinte	*veent*
6	seis	*saheesh*	21	vinte e um/a	*veent ee oõm /**oo**mah*
7	sete	*set*			
8	oito	*o**hee**too*			
9	nove	*nov*	22	vinte e dois, duas	*veent ee doheesh/ **doo**ahsh*
10	dez	*desh*			
11	onze	*ohñz*			
12	doze	*dohz*	30	trinta	***treeñ**tah*
13	treze	*trehz*			

40	quarenta	*kwarehñ-tah*	201	duzentos/as e um/a	*doozehñ-toosh/ahsh ee ooñ/oomah*
50	cinquenta	*seeñ-kwehñtah*			
60	sessenta	*susehñtah*	300	trezentos/as	*truzehñ-toosh/ahsh*
70	setenta	*setehñtah*			
80	oitenta	*oheetehñ-tah*	400	quatrocen-tos/as	*kwatroo sêhntoosh/ahsh*
90	noventa	*noovehñ-tah*	500	quinhentos/as	*keen-nyehñ-toosh/ahsh*
100	cem, cento	*sehñ, sehñtoo*			
101	cento e um/a	*sehñtoo ee ooñ/oomah*	600	seiscentos/as	*saheesh-sehñtoosh/ahsh*
110	cento e dez	*sehñtoo ee desh*	700	setecentos/as	*setsehn-toosh/ahsh*
200	duzentos/as	*doozehñ-toosh/ahsh*	800	oitocentos/as	*oheetoo-sehntoosh/ahsh*
			900	novecentos/as	*novsehn-toosh/ahsh*

1.000	mil	*meel*
2.000	dois mil	*doheesh meel*
1.000.000	um milhão	*ooñ meellãhoo*
2.000.000	dois milhões	*doheesh meelloheensh*

check out 3

You go to the bank to change some money.

- ○ Bom dia.
  *bohm **dee**ah*

- Bom dia. Qual é o câmbio da libra?
  *bohm **dee**ah. kwal e oo **kah**m̃beeoo dah **lee**brah*

- ○ A um euro e quarenta e oito.
  *ah oom̃ **e**roo ee kwah**rehñ**tah ee **ohee**too*

- Queria trocar cem libras.
  *ku**ree**a troo**kar** sehm̃ **lee**brahsh*

- ○ Muito bem. O passaporte, se faz favor.
  mooeeñ**too baheem̃. oo pasah**port** su fash fah**vohr

Q How much do you want to change?

countries & nationalities

Australia, Australian	a Austrália, australiano/a	*ah aooshtraleeah, aooshtrahleeahnoo/ah*
Brazil, Brazilian	o Brasil, brasileiro/a	*oo brahzeel, brahzeelaheeroo/ah*
Canada, Canadian	o Canadá, canadense	*oo kahnahda, kanahdehnsu*
England, English	a Inglaterra, inglês/esa	*ah eenglahterrah, eenglehsh/ehzah*
Great Britain, British	a Grã-Bretanha, britânico/a	*ah gran brehtāneeah, breetāneecoo/ah*
(Northern) Ireland, Northern Irish/Irish	a Irlanda (do Norte), da Irlanda do Norte/ irlandês/esa	*ah eerlahndah (doo nort), dah eerlahndah doo nort, eerlahndehsh/ehzah*
Portugal, Portuguese	Portugal, português/esa	*poortoogal, poortoogehsh/ehzah*
Scotland, Scottish	a Escócia, escocês/esa	*ah eeshkoseeah, eeshkooehsh/ehzah*
South Africa, South African	a África do Sul, sul-africano/a	*ah afreekah doo sool, soolahfreekahnoo/ah*
United States, American	os Estados Unidos, americano/a	*oosh eeshtadoosh ooneedoosh, amureekahnoo/ah*
Wales, Welsh	o País de Gales, galês/esa	*oo paheesh du galush gahlehsh/ehzah*

days

Monday	segunda-feira	*sugooñdah faheerah*
Tuesday	terça-feira	*tehrsah faheerah*
Wednesday	quarta-feira	*kwartah faheerah*
Thursday	quinta-feira	*keeñtah faheerah*
Friday	sexta-feira	*sehshtah faheerah*
Saturday	sábado	*sabahdoo*
Sunday	domingo	*doomeeñgoo*
today	hoje	*ohj*
yesterday	ontem	*ohntaheeñ*
tomorrow	amanhã	*amahñnyāh*

months

January	Janeiro	*jah**nahee**roo*
February	Fevereiro	*fuvu**rahee**roo*
March	Março	***mar**soo*
April	Abril	*ah**breel***
May	Maio	***maee**oo*
June	Junho	***joo**ñnyoo*
July	Julho	***joo**lloo*
August	Agosto	*ah**gohsh**too*
September	Setembro	*su**tehm̃**broo*
October	Outubro	*oh**too**broo*
November	Novembro	*noo**vem̃**broo*
December	Dezembro	*du**zehm̃**broo*

sound check

Portuguese has a nasal sound when a vowel has a 'til' (~) over it. E.g. não sounds like a long drawn-out 'now', said through your nose.

The nasal sounds also occurs when a vowel is followed by **m** or **n**, often at the end of a word. E.g. tem sounds like a long drawn-out 'tame', said through your nose.

tem *taheem̃*   sim *seem̃*

Practise the sound in these words:

são *sãhoo*   bem *baheem̃*
bom *bohm̃*   cem *sehm̃*
um *oom̃*   custam ***koosh**tahm̃*

Bare **Necessities**

try it out

lucky numbers

Write down these numbers in Portuguese. The first one has been done for you.

23 – vinte e três	5	15	125
39	51	311	1000

lost in translation

How would you say the following sentences in Portuguese?

1 I work in London.
2 I speak English and Portuguese.
3 Sorry!
4 Where is the lift?
5 I would like a coffee. (coffee is um café, *oom kahfe*)
6 How much is the book? (book is o livro, *oo leevroo*)
7 I don't understand.

as if you were there

You're sitting at the bar in the hotel, when another guest starts talking to you. Follow the prompts to play your part.

Boa noite. Chamo-me Carlos.
(Say your name is Anna)
É inglesa?
(Say yes, you're from Wimbledon)
Está em Portugal de férias?
(Say no, you're on business)
Quanto tempo está em Portugal?
(Say you are in Portugal for two days)

linkup

key phrases

Há sanitários?	Are there any toilets?
Tem gelado?	Do you have ice cream?
Queria cem gramas.	I'd like a hundred grammes.
Dê-me dois quilos.	I'll have two kilos.
Onde é a estação?	Where's the station?
Sou inglês/inglesa.	I'm English.
Chamo-me/ O meu nome é ...	My name is ...
Moro em York.	I live in York.
Tenho dois filhos.	I have two children.

listening & replying

When people ask you questions about yourself, such as Tem filhos? (Do you have children?) it's tempting to reply using the same word: tem.

But instead, make sure you change the form of the word, using tenho (I have) not tem (you have):
Sim, tenho dois filhos./Não, não tenho filhos.
Yes, I have two children./No, I don't have children.

Some other common questions and possible replies:
Onde mora? – Moro em Southend.
Where do you live? – I live in Southend.
Como se chama? – Chamo-me David.
What's your name? – My name is David.

Bare **Necessities**

missing words

Because the form of the verb tells you who is being referred to, it is very common not to use the words for 'I' (eu) or 'you' (o senhor/a senhora/você) in Portuguese:

Sou inglês. (not Eu sou ...) I'm English.
Moro em Southend. (not Eu moro ...) I live in Southend.
Tem filhos? (not O senhor tem ...) Do you have children?

The same applies to the words for 'he', 'she' and 'it' (ele and ela):

Como se chama a sua filha? – Chama-se Sara. What's your daughter called? – She's called Sara. (not Ela chama-se ...)

Onde é o elevador? – É à direita. Where is the lift? – It's on the right. (not Ele é à ...)

For more on pronouns, see the Language Builder, p135. ·····>

the way you say things

You can't always transfer expressions word for word from English to Portuguese:

For example, Chamo-me David literally means '(I) call myself David', but translates as 'My name is David'.
So often it pays to learn the whole phrase rather than the individual words.

numbers

Note that the words for one, two and the hundreds change in Portuguese, depending on the word they are referring to.

For more on how they change, see the Language Builder: articles, p129, and adjectives, p130. ·····>

Getting **Around**

driving in Portugal

You can hire a car in all main airports and in most major towns and resorts. If arranged prior to travel, check whether there is a fee for having the car delivered to the airport.

Portugal has been investing in its roads, and it's worth paying to travel on the fast A-roads, especially between Lisbon and Porto and across the Algarve.

Remember that Portugal has a notoriously high accident rate, due to a combination of the poor state of many roads, fast driving and reckless overtaking. In towns, parking centrally can be difficult, while congestion in Porto and Lisbon is particularly bad.

A roads Toll roads, generally fast and uncrowded dual carriageways with regular service stations. Speed limit: usually 75mph.

IP roads Fast roads, much the same as A roads but without the tolls so tend to be much more crowded.

IC/EN Major main roads, usually with one lane each way and sections of dual carriageway. Often busy.; watch out for slow lorries. Speed limit: 56mph.

N roads Main roads, usually one lane each way, often busy but the best way to see Portuguese towns and villages. Slow local traffic can include horses and carts. Speed limit: 56mph/31mph in urban areas.

coaches & buses

Portugal is not a big country, and if you plan to visit just major towns, you'll find the various privately run **camioneta** (coach) and **autocarro** (bus) services a reliable and efficient way to travel. Larger towns have a central bus station where you can get tickets and timetables; otherwise, check in the tourist office or a central café. Usually you pay on the bus. In more remote places, such as between smaller villages in Beira Alta/Baixa and Trás-os-Montes, services can be very infrequent.

trains

Regional The slowest local trains which stop at all stations. Usually extremely cheap.

Inter-regional Slightly faster than **Regionaís** although they cost the same, these stop at intermediate stations only.

Intercidade These faster inter-city trains cost slightly more.

Alfa The most expensive but quickest service from Lisbon to Coimbra and Porto. Make sure you buy tickets in advance.

For more information on the **serviços** (services) and **horários** (times) check out the **Comboios Portugueses** website: **www.cp.pt**.

Train travel can be a fantastic way to see the Portuguese countryside. Some unmissable rail routes include: the breezy coastal route from Porto to Valença (three hours) via Viana do Castelo; the scenic inland river valley route from Porto to Amarante (two hours); Porto to Régua, through port wine-growing country along the Douro (two hours); Régua to Vila Real in Trás-os-Montes (an hour), a tiny one-track train following a steep river valley, passing through vineyards and back gardens.

train tickets

Buy a ticket before boarding. Children under twelve usually pay half price while those under four travel free. Over 65s pay a reduced fee. A **cartão de família** (family rail pass) is good value, and a **bilhete turístico** (tourist rail pass) is worthwhile if you plan to make a lot of train journeys; valid for one, two or three weeks.

city transport

Taxis use meters in towns, but once outside the urban boundaries the fare is charged by the kilometre. Expect to pay around €1.50 for luggage regardless of weight or number.

Metro Services in Lisbon and Oporto, which run from 6am-1am.

Trams and funiculars The British-made pre-war **eléctricos**

(trams) are amongst Porto's and Lisbon's most distinctive features, the perfect way to negotiate steep and narrow hills. To identify tram stops, follow the overhead power lines and look for the Carris company sign. Carris also runs Lisbon's **elevadores** (funiculars).

Cycling is growing in popularity, especially around the flat coastal areas. Ask in the local tourist office for bike hire companies. You can take your bike on some trains, and off-peak it may be free.

tickets & passes

With all forms of public transport, make sure you **oblitere** (punch) your ticket before your journey to validate it, or face a fine. In train stations and on the metro, machines are just before the platforms. On trams and buses they are just inside the door. If you plan to take a few journeys, it works out cheaper to buy books of 10 tickets from newsagents or city kiosks. You can also buy one- or five-day bus passes or bus/underground combined passes.

ferries

A **ferry-boat** service links Lisbon with the south of the river Tagus at Cacilhas or Montijo, and Setúbal over the river Sado with the Tróia peninsula, offering a scenic, if leisurely, route south.

Catch the summer ferry from Peniche to the Atlantic Berlenga islands, a popular destination for campers and bird watchers.

phrasemaker

asking the way

you may say ...

Excuse me! (to attract attention)	Desculpe!	*dush**koolp***
Which way is ...	Para ...	*pah**rah***
the beach?	a praia?	*ah **prae**eah*
the town centre?	o centro da cidade?	*oo **sehn**troo dah see**da**du*
the port?	o porto?	*oo **pohr**too*
the Tourist Office?	o Posto de Turismo?	*oo **pohsh**too du too**reesh**moo*
Is there ... near here?	Há ... perto daqui?	*a ... **per**too dah**kee***
a bank	um banco	*ooм̃ **bahñ**koo*
an internet cafe	um café internet	*ooм̃ kah**fe** eenter**net***
a bus stop	uma paragem de autocarro	***oo**mah pah**ra**jaheeм̃ du aooto**ka**rroo*
Are there any large shops near here?	Há lojas grandes perto daqui?	*a **lo**jahsh **grahñ**dush **per**too dah**kee***
Where is ...	Onde fica ...	*ohnd **fee**kah*
the castle?	o castelo?	*oo kahsh**te**loo*
the bus/train/metro station?	a estação de autocarros/caminho de ferro/metro?	*ah eeshtah**sãhoo** du aooto**ka**rroosh/ kah**meen**nyoo du **fe**rroo/**me**tro*
Is it far?	Fica longe?	***fee**kah **lohn**j*
I'm lost!	Estou perdido/a.	*eesht**oh** per**dee**do/ah*

you may hear ...

Aí (é).	*ah**ee** (e)*	There (it is).
Sempre em frente.	*sehm**pru** ahee**м̃**frehnt*	Carry straight on.
Vire à direita/ esquerda.	*vee**ru** a dee**rahee**tah/ eesh**kehr**dah*	Turn right/left.

Atravesse ...	ahtrah**ve**su	Cross ...
a ponte.	ah pohnt	the bridge.
a estrada principal.	ah eesh**tra**dah preensee**pal**	the main road.
À ...	a	On the ...
direita.	dee**ra**heetah	right.
esquerda.	eesh**kehr**dah	left.
a primeira/segunda rua	ah pree**mahee**rah/ su**goon**dah **rroo**ah	the first/second street
Até ao largo/à praça.	ah**te** aoo **lar**goo/a **pra**sah	As far as the square.
a cem metros.	ah sehm̃**me**troosh	100 metres away
Fica a uns trinta quilómetros.	**fee**kah ah oonsh **treen**tah kee**lo**mutroosh	It's about 30km away.
É (bastante) ...	e (bash**tahnt**)	It's (fairly) ...
perto.	**per**too	close.
longe.	lohnj	far away.
perto/em frente/ atrás	**per**too/aheem̃ frehnt/ ah**trash**	near/opposite/ behind
no fim da rua	noo feem̃dah **rroo**ah	at the end of the street
na esquina	nah eesh**kee**nah	on the corner

(For shops see p57, and for places to visit see p103.)

check out 1

A passer-by helps you get to the cathedral.

○ Para a catedral?
 pahrah ah kahtu**dral**

- É na segunda rua à esquerda. Fica no fim.
 e nah su**goon**dah **rroo**ah a eesh**kehr**dah. **fee**kah noo feem̃

Q You have to take the second street on the right: true or false?

hiring a car or bike

you may say ...

I'd like to hire a ... 　car. 　motorbike. 　bike.	Queria alugar ... 　um carro. 　uma motocicleta. 　uma bicicleta.	*kureeah ahloogar* 　*ooñ **ka**rroo* 　***oo**mah 　motosee**kle**tah* 　***oo**mah beesee**kle**tah*
a ... car 　small 　medium 　large	um carro ... 　pequeno 　médio 　grande	*ooñ **ka**rroo* 　*pu**keh**noo* 　***me**deeoo* 　*grahnd*
How much does it cost per day/week?	Quanto é por dia/ semana?	***kwahñ**too e poor **dee**ah/su**mah**nah*
Is insurance included?	Está incluído o seguro?	*ee**shta** eenkloo**ee**do oo su**goo**roo*

you may hear ...

Por quanto tempo?	*poor **kwahñ**too **tehm**poo*	For how long?
Custa quarenta euros por dia.	*koosh*tah kwa**rehñ**tah e*roosh poor **dee**ah*	It costs €40 euros per day. (See numbers, p14)
A sua carta de condução, se faz favor.	*ah **sooa** **kar**tah du cohndoo**sãhoo** su fash fah**vohr***	Your driving licence, please.
Cobramos entrega.	*koo**brah**moosh ehn**tre**gah*	We charge delivery.
O sinal é ...	*oo see**nal** e*	The deposit is ...

getting petrol

you may say ...

Where is the ...	Onde está ...	*ohnd eeshta*
unleaded?	a sem chumbo?	*ah saheeñ **shoom**boo*
4-star?	a super?	*ah **soo**per*
diesel?	o gasóleo?	*oo ga**zo**leeoo*
Can you check ...	Pode verificar ...	*pod vehreefee**kar***
the air?	o ar?	*ar*
the oil?	o óleo?	***ol**eo*
Do you have ...	Tem ...	*taheeñ*
water?	água?	***a**gooah*
maps?	mapas?	***ma**pahsh*

you may hear...

É auto-serviço.	*e **aoo**to sur**vee**soo*	It is self-service.
Bomba numéro quatro.	***bom**ba **noo**meroo **kwa**troo*	Pump number 4.

on the road

you may say ...

Where are we on the map?	Onde ficamos no mapa?	*ohnd fee**kah**moosh noo **ma**pah*
How far is Lisbon?	A quantos quilómetros fica Lisboa?	*ah **kwahñt**oosh kee**lo**mutroosh **fee**kah leesh**boh**ah*
Can I park here?	Posso estacionar aqui?	***po**soo eeshtahseeoo**nar** ah**kee***
Where is the car park?	Onde fica o parque de estacionamento?	*ohnd **fee**kah oo park du eeshtahseeoonah-**mehn**too*
Is this the road to Porto?	É este o caminho para o Porto?	*e ehsht oo kah**mee**ñyoo **pah**rah oo **por**too*

28

Getting **Around**

road signs
you may see ...

acenda os faróis	use headlights
autoestrada	motorway
dê prioridade	give priority
desvio	diversion
devagar	slowly
estacionamento permitido	parking allowed
proibido estacionar	parking forbidden
mantenha-se pela direita	keep right
não ultrapassar	no overtaking
norte/sul/este/oeste	north/south/east/west
obras	road works
peagem/portagem	toll
perigo	danger
sem saída	no through road
sentido proibido	no access
zona para peões	pedestrian zone

check out 2
You stop for petrol and to check directions.

○ Onde está a sem chumbo?
*ohnd eeshta ah saheem **shoom**boo*

- É ali. Número quatro.
*e ah**lee**. **noo**meroo **kwa**troo*

○ É este o caminho para Évora?
*E **eh**sht oo kah**meen**nyoo **pah**rah evoorah*

- É, sim. Fica a uns trinta quilómetros.
*e seem. **fee**kah ah oonsh **treen**tah kee**lo**mutroosh*

Q You are going the wrong way: true or false?

29

using the underground

you may say …

Two tickets, please.	Dois bilhetes, se faz favor.	*doheesh beellehtush su fash fahvohr*
A book of ten, please.	Uma caderneta de dez, se faz favor.	*oomah kahdurnehtah du desh su fash fahvohr*
Does this train go to …?	Este metro vai para …?	*ehsht metroo vaee pahrah*
Is there access for … wheelchairs?	Há acesso para … cadeiras de rodas?	*a ahsesoo pahrah kahdaheerahsh du rodahsh*
prams?	carrinhos de bebé?	*kahrreennyoosh du bebe*

you may hear …

Tome a linha/ o número …	*tom ah leeñnyah/ oo noomuroo*	Take line/number …
Tem de mudar/ descer na próxima paragem.	*taheem du moodar/ dushsehr na proseema pahrajaheem*	You need to change/ get off at the next stop.

getting information

you may say …

Are there … to? buses trains flights	Há … para? autocarros comboios voos	*a … pahrah aootokarroosh kohmboeeoosh vohoosh*
What time is the boat/plane to …?	A que horas é o barco/avião para …?	*ah ku orahsh e oo barkoo/ahveeãhoo pahrah*
What time is the next one?	A que horas é o próximo?	*ah ku orahsh e oo proseemoo*
Does this train go to …?	Este comboio vai para …?	*ehsht kohmboeeoo vaee pahrah*
Is it direct?	É directo?	*e deeretoo*

Where is the connection?	Onde é a ligação?	*ohnd e ah leegah**sãhoo***
From which platform?	De que cais/linha?	*du ku kaeesh/**leeñnyah***
At what time does it arrive?	A que horas chega?	*ah ku **o**rahsh **she**hgah*
How long does it take?	Quanto tempo demora?	***kwahn**too **tehm**poo du**mo**rah*
When does the last one come back?	A que horas regressa o último?	*ah ku **o**rahsh rru**gre**sah oo **ool**teemoo*
Have you got a timetable?	Tem a tabela de horários?	*taheeñ ah tah**be**lah dee o**ra**reeoosh*
Can you tell me where to get off?	Pode avisar-me onde devo descer?	*pod ahvee**zar**-mu ohnd **deh**voo du**shsehr***

you may hear …

Desça/Mude em …	***dehsh**sah/**moo**du aheeñ*	Get off/Change at …
Transporte grátis de bicicletas.	*transh**port gra**teesh du beeseek**le**tahsh*	Bicycles go free.

buying a ticket

you may say ...

Where is the ticket office?	Onde é a bilheteira?	*ohnd e ah beellutaheerah*
A return ticket, please.	Um bilhete de ida e volta, se faz favor.	*oõm beellehtu du eedah ee voltah su fash fahvohr*
A single ticket, to ...	Um bilhete simples, para ...	*oõm beellehtu seemplush pahrah*
for two adults and one child	para dois adultos e uma criança	*pahrah doheesh ahdooltoosh ee oomah kreeahnsah*
first/second class	primeira/segunda classe	*preemaheerah/ sugoondah klasu*
a tourist rail pass	um bilhete turístico	*oõm beellehtu tooreeshteekoo*
I'd like to reserve ... a seat. a couchette.	Queria reservar ... um lugar. uma couchette.	*kureeah rruzurvar oõm loogar oomah kooshet*
Is there a reduction for ... young people? disabled travellers? senior citizens?	Tem desconto para ... jovens? deficientes? idosos?	*taheem duskontu pahrah jovuñsh dufeeseeehñtush eedozush*

you may hear ...

| Fumadores ou não fumadores? | *foomahdohrush oh nãhoo foomahdohrush* | Smoking or non-smoking? |

Há um suplemento de ...	*a ooṁ sooplu**mehn**too du*	There is a supplement of ...
Oblitere/Valide o seu bilhete.	*ob**lee**teru/vah**lee**d oo **seh**oo bee**lleh**t*	Punch/Validate your ticket.

signs
you may see ...

alfândega	customs
chegadas	arrivals
controlo de passaportes	passport control
depósito de bagagens	left-luggage
entrada	entrance
partidas	departures
perdidos e achados	lost property
porta/portão	gate
saída	exit
sala de espera	waiting room

check out 3
You are planning a day out in the countryside.

○ Há autocarros para Loulé?
*a aooto**karr**oosh **pah**rah loh**le***

- Há, sim. Há um cada hora.
*a seeṁ. a ooṁ **kah**dah **o**rah*

○ A que horas regressa o último?
*ah ku **o**rahsh rru**gre**sah oo **ool**teemoo*

- Às sete horas.
*ash set **o**rahsh*

(cada hora = every hour)

Q   What time is the last bus?

taking a taxi
you may say …

Is there a taxi rank round here?	Há uma praça de táxis perto daqui?	a **oo**mah **pra**sah du **tak**seesh **per**too dah**kee**
To …, please.	Para …, se faz favor.	**pah**rah … su fash fah**vohr**
the airport	o aeroporto	oo aero**pohr**too
the station	a estação	ah eshtah**sãhoo**
the castle	o castelo	oo kash**te**loo
this address	este endereço	ehsht ehndu**reh**soo
How long will it take?	Quanto tempo demora?	**kwahñ**too **tehm**poo du**mor**ah
How far is it?	A que distância é?	ah ku deesh**tahñ**seeah e
Stop here.	Pare aqui.	**pa**ru ah**kee**
How much …	Quanto …	**kwahñ**too
is that?	é?	e
will it be?	será?	su**ra**

I'd like a receipt.	Queria um recibo.	*ku**ree**ah oom* *rru**see**boo*
Keep the change.	Guarde o troco.	*gooard oo **troh**koo*
This is for you. (See p132 for 'you')	Isto é para o senhor/a senhora.	*eeshtoo e **pah**rah oo sunny**ohr**/ ah sunny**oh**rah*

you may hear ...

não demora muito	*nãhoo du**mo**rah moo**een**too*	not long
não é longe	*nãhoo e lohnj*	not far

check out 4

You jump in a taxi to the airport.

○ Para a estação, se faz favor. É longe?
*pahrah ah eeshtah**sãhoo** su fash fahvohr. e lohnj*

- Não é longe. Fica a dez minutos.
*nãhoo e lohnj. **fee**kah a desh meen**oo**toosh*

 Your train leaves in 20 minutes – will you make it in time?

sound check

g followed by **e** or **i** and **j** both have the same sound – they are pronounced like the 's' in 'pleasure':

longe *lohnj*   laranjas *lahrahñjahsh*

paragem *pahrajaheem*   loja *lojah*

lost for words

K	L	B	D	E	A	N	A	P	L
L	O	I	G	C	A	R	R	O	U
H	U	C	N	N	N	O	R	C	M
A	V	I	A	O	A	R	H	R	O
I	I	C	X	I	A	T	A	A	I
O	P	L	C	C	C	R	O	B	O
R	L	E	O	O	O	E	R	L	B
E	A	T	J	F	T	P	T	O	M
Q	U	A	J	F	T	O	E	G	O
A	W	L	O	N	G	E	M	O	C

There are eight types of transport hidden here. Words go up and down, backwards, forwards and diagonally.

location, location, location

All these words for places around a town have been broken up. Can you match the beginnings with the ends?

ban	cast	pra	esta	pra	lar	cate
ça	ia	co	dral	ção	go	elo

as if you were there

You're in the train station, making a booking at the ticket office. Follow the prompts to play your part.

(Ask for two return tickets to Óbidos)
Dezassete euros.

(Ask what time the train arrives)
Às duas horas.

(Ask whether it is a direct train)
Não. Mude em Sintra.

(Say thank you)

linkup

Onde é/fica a catedral?	**Where is** the cathedral?
É/Fica longe?	**Is it** far?
Há um museu?	**Is there** a museum?
Tem uma planta da cidade?	**Do you have** a plan of the town?
Queria alugar um carro.	**I'd like** to hire a car.
A que horas abre?	**What time** does it open?
Para o aeroporto.	**To/For** the airport.

how to ask a question

Sometimes questions are easy, because they follow the same pattern as in English:

Quanto é isto? How much is this?
Há um banco perto daqui? Is there a bank near here?

But sometimes the word order is different:

Está incluído o seguro? Is insurance included?
A que horas regressa o último? What time does the last one come back?

Notice that Portuguese has no equivalent of the English use of 'do' or 'does' in questions.

For more on asking questions see the Language Builder, p136. ⋯⋯▷

saying where things are

Two very useful phrases when you're travelling:

É longe. It's a long way.
É perto. It's close.

When you're saying what a place is near to or far from, use
da (if the word that follows is feminine) or **do** (if the word that
follows is masculine):

É longe **da** cidade. It's a long way **from the** town.
É perto **do** mercado. It's near **to the** market.

When you're saying how far in time or distance, use **a**:
É **a** dois quilómetros. It's two kilometres away.
É **a** dez minutos daqui. It's ten minutes away.

to be – ser & ficar

When describing where things are in Portuguese, you can use
one of two verbs: ser or ficar.

Ser means 'to be' and is used when talking about something
with a permanent state, for example a building:

Onde **é** o banco? Where **is** the bank?
Os sanitários **são** a cinco minutos. The toilets **are** five
minutes away.

Fica means 'to be (found)', and can also be used when talking
about locations:

Onde **fica** o castelo? Where **is** the castle?
As lojas **ficam** perto. The shops **are (found)** nearby.

For more on the verb 'to be', see the Language Builder,
p134.

Somewhere to **Stay**

Portugal has a wide range of places to stay, but it's a good idea to book ahead over the busy summer months. For help planning where and when to go see: **www.visitportugal.com** or **www.portugal.org**.

If you plan to find accommodation when you're there, local tourist offices can provide details and check availability for you.

Children under two are usually free and those under 12 may be half-price in hotels if sharing a room with adults. Check beforehand to arrange cots or discuss any particular access requirements.

hotels

One- to three-star hotels are good value; rooms usually have a television and ensuite bathroom, and prices normally include breakfast. For a more luxurious stay, four- and five-star hotels, along with **estalagens** and **albergarias** (inns), offer all the usual facilities of a high-end hotel.

pousadas

Pousadas are up-market hotels, often in beautifully converted historic buildings, from castles (such as in Óbidos), to monasteries (such as in Évora). Though expensive, they are worth it for the unique settings and good-quality restaurants.

country houses

Privately-let country and manor houses offer visitors another chance to stay in traditional buildings full of character. These vary from simple farm buildings to lavish mansions. Breakfast is included, and you can often choose to have an evening meal with the host family.

guesthouses

A **pensão** is a privately-run guesthouse graded by the tourist board. Room prices should be displayed on the back of each bedroom door. Facilities vary

widely; the better ones are ensuite and as good as many hotels, with substantial breakfasts included. Others are much more basic, with shared bathrooms or even just a jug of water and a basin, but cheap.

Other, cheaper, variants are the **residencial**, or the slightly more basic **hospedaria/casa de hóspedes** (hostel).

Another option is to stay in a room in a private house. Look for windows displaying signs saying **quartos** or **dormidas**. Make sure you see the room before you take it, and agree on a price beforehand. Prices should work out cheaper than **pensões**.

self-catering

With excellent fresh food available from markets, self-catering can be an attractive option. Ask the Portuguese tourist board for lists of self-catering apartments (rated two- to five-stars) and villas (three- to five-stars) throughout Portugal. Self-catering is particularly prevalent in the Algarve, with apartments and villas for large groups. Check transport connections if you don't have a car.

camping & hostels

If you have an HI card, you can stay in a **pousada de juventude** (youth hostel), some of which are in great locations, although price-wise they are little cheaper than staying in a **pensão**.

If you want to stay in some of Portugal's beauty spots, there are several good-value campsites (rated one- to four-stars). These can get busy in the summer months. Some campsites are classified as public, i.e. open to all paying campers, others are private, meaning you need to be a member. For a list of campsites see: **www.roteiro-campista.pt**.

phrasemaker

finding a place
you may say ...

Is there a ... near here?	Há ... aqui perto?	a ... ah**kee per**too
hotel	um hotel	oo**ñ** o**tel**
campsite	um parque de campismo	oo**ñ** **park** du kam**pee**shmoo
youth hostel	uma pousada de juventude	**oo**mah poh**za**dah du joovehn**too**d
flat to let	um apartamento para alugar	oo**ñ** ahpahrtah**mehn**too **pah**rah ahloo**gar**
Do you have a ... room?	Tem um quarto ...	ta**heeñ** oo**ñ** **kwar**too
single	individual?	eendeeveedoo**al**
double	duplo?	**doo**ploo
family	para uma família?	**pah**rah **oo**mah fah**mee**leeah
for ...	para ...	**pah**rah
two nights	duas noites	**doo**ahsh no**hee**tush
four people	quatro pessoas	**kwa**troo pu**soh**ahss
two adults and two children	dois adultos e duas crianças	doheesh ah**dool**toosh ee **doo**ahsh kreeah**ñ**sahsh
(See numbers, p14)		
May I see the room?	Posso ver o quarto?	**po**soo vehr oo **kwar**too
How much is it per night?	Quanto é por noite?	**kwahñ**too e poor no**heet**
Don't you have anything cheaper?	Não tem nada mais barato?	nã**hoo** ta**heeñ** **na**dah ma**eesh** bah**ra**too
Is there a discount for children?	Tem desconto para crianças?	ta**heeñ** dus**kon**tu **pah**rah kreeah**ñ**sahsh
I'll take it.	Fico com ele.	**fee**koo koh**ñ**ehl
I'll let you know.	Ainda não sei.	ah**eeñ**dah nã**hoo** sahee

Quantas noites/pessoas?	*kwahñtash noheetush/pusohahsh*	How many nights/people?
Lamento, o hotel está cheio.	*lahmehñtoo oo otel eeshta shaheeoo*	I'm sorry, the hotel is full.
As crianças pagam metade.	*ahsh kreeahnsahsh pagahoom mutadu*	Children are half-price.

check out 1

You are asking for a room in a hotel.

○ Tem um quarto duplo?
  *taheeṁ ooṁ **kwar**too **doo**ploo*

- Quantas noites?
  ***kwahñ**tahsh **nohee**tush*

○ Para três noites.
  ***pah**rah trehsh **nohee**tush*

Q Do you want a single or double room?
What does the receptionist ask?

checking in

you may say ...

I have a reservation.	Tenho uma reserva.	*tahñnyoo rruzurva*
My name is ...	Chamo-me ...	*shahmoo-mu*
Where can I park?	Onde posso estacionar?	*ohnd posoo eeshtahseeoonar*

Somewhere to **Stay**

you may hear ...

Qual é ... o seu nome? a matrícula do seu carro?	kwal e oo sehoo nohm ah mah**tree**koolah doo sehoo **ka**rroo	What is ... your name? your car registration number?
Posso ver o seu passaporte?	**po**soo vehr oo **se**hoo pasah**port**	May I see your passport?
Queira preencher esta ficha, se faz favor.	ka**hee**rah preeehn**shehr esh**tah **fee**shah su fash fah**vohr**	Please fill in the form.
O quarto número ...	oo **kwar**too **noo**muroo	Room number ...

asking about your room
you may say ...

with ... bathroom shower cot balcony	com ... casa de banho duche cama de bebé varanda	kohm̃ **ka**zah du **bah**ñnyo doosh **kah**mah du be**be** vah**rahn**dah
with a single/ double bed	com uma cama individual/de casal	kohm̃ **oo**mah **kah**mah eendeeveedoo**al**/ du ka**zal**
Is breakfast included?	Está incluído o pequeno almoço?	eesh**ta** eenkloo**ee**doo oo pu**keh**noo al**moh**soo
Is value-added tax included?	Está incluído o IVA?	eesh**ta** eenkloo**ee**doo oo **ee**vah
Does the room have ... an internet point? a view?	O quarto tem ... ligação à internet? vista?	oo **kwar**too taheem̃ leegah**sāh**oo a eenter**net** **veesh**tah
Is there access for wheelchairs?	Há acesso para cadeiras de rodas?	a ah**seh**soo **pah**rah kah**deh**reerash du **rro**dahahsh

you may hear ...

meia pensão	*maheeah pehnsãhoo*	half board
O pequeno almoço/ IVA ...	*oo pukehnoo almohsoo/eevah*	Breakfast/Tax ...
está incluído.	*eeshta eenklueedo*	is included.
não está incluído.	*nãhoo eeshta eenklueedo*	is not included.

check out 2

You're asking the price of a room.

○ Quanto é por noite?
kwahñtoo e poor noheet

- Noventa e oito euros.
noovehnta ee oheeto eroosh

○ Não tem nada mais barato?
nãhoo taheeñ nadah maheesh bahratoo

- Não, senhor.
nãhoo suññyohr

○ Fico com ele.
feekoo kohñehl

Q How much will you have to pay for this room?

services

you may say ...

What time is breakfast?	A que horas é o pequeno almoço?	*ah ku **o**rahsh e oo pu**keh**noo al**moh**soo*

Is there a ...
  lift?
  gym?
  laundry/room service?
	Há ...
	  elevador?
	  ginásio?
	  serviço de lavandaria/quartos?
		*a
		  eeluvah**dohr**
		  jee**na**zeeoo
		  sur**vee**soo du lahvahndah**ree**ah/ **kwar**toosh*

Where is ...
  the restaurant?
  the bar?
  the garden?
	Onde é ...
	  o restaurante
	  o bar?
	  o jardim?
		*ohnd e
		  oo rushtaoo**rahn**t
		  oo bar
		  oo jahr**deeñ***

How do I get an outside line?	Como marco uma ligação exterior?	*kohmoo **mar**koo **oo**mah leegah**sãhoo** aheeshturee**ohr***

you may hear ...

Das sete e meia às dez e meia.	*dahsh set ee **mahee**ah ash desh ee **mahee**ah*	From 7.30 to 10.30. (See times, p14)
no primeiro/segundo ander	*noo pree**mahee**eroo/ sug**oon**doo ahn**dar***	on the first/second floor
É ao lado da piscina.	*e aoo **la**doo dah peesh**see**nah*	It's next to the swimming pool.
Marque zero.	*mark **ze**roo*	Dial zero.

asking for help

you may say ...

... isn't working.	... não funciona.	... *nãhoo foonseeohnah*
The telephone	O telefone	*oo tulufon*
The shower	O duche	*oo doosh*
The light	A luz	*ah loosh*
There is a problem with ...	Há um problema com ...	*a oõm prooblehmah kohm*
the television.	a televisão.	*ah tuluveezãhoo*
the lamp.	a lâmpada.	*ah lahmpahdah*
the window.	a janela.	*ah jahnelah*
How do you work the air conditioning?	Como funciona o ar condicionado?	*kohmoo foonseeohnah oo ar kohndeeseeoonadoo*
There is no ...	Não há ...	*nãhoo a*
soap.	sabonete.	*sahbooneht*
hot/cold water.	água quente/fria.	*agooah kehnt/ freeah*
toilet paper.	papel higiénico.	*pahpel eejeeeneekoo*
There are no ...	Não há ...	*nãhoo a*
towels.	toalhas.	*tooallahsh*
pillows.	almofadas.	*almoofadahsh*
blankets.	cobertores.	*kooburtohrush*
Do you have ...	Tem ...	*taheem*
a safe-deposit box?	cofre/caixa forte?	*kofru/kaheeshah fort*
an iron?	ferro de engomar?	*ferroo du ehngoomar oomah plahntah*
a plan of the town?	uma planta da vila?	*dah veelah*
Could you order me a taxi?	Pode-me chamar um táxi?	*podu-mu shahmar oõm taksee*
I'd like an alarm call at ...	Queria uma chamada para acordar-me às ...	*kureeah oomah shahmadah pahrah ahkoordar-mu ash*

you may hear ...

Mando alguém.	*mahñdoo algaheem*	I'll send somebody.
Vou buscá-los/las.	*voh booshkaloosh/ laash*	I'll get you them.

46

checking out
you may say ...

I'd like to pay the bill.	Queria pagar a conta.	*ku**ree**ah pah**gar** ah* **kohñ**tah
by credit card	com cartão de crédito	*kohm̃ kahr**tãhoo** du* **kre**deetoo
in cash	em dinheiro	*aheem̃* *deeñ**nyahee**roo*
I think there is a mistake.	Creio que se enganou na conta.	*kra**hee**oo ku su* *ehngah**noh** na* **kohñ**tah

you may hear ...

Qual é o número do seu quarto?	*kwal e oo **noo**muroo doo **seh**oo **kwar**too*	What is your room number?
Como vai pagar?	**koh**moo vaee pah**gar**	How are you going to pay?
Assine aqui.	*ah**see**nu ah**kee***	Sign here.

check out 3
You're settling your bill at reception.

- ○ Queria pagar a conta.
  *ku**ree**ah pah**gar** ah **kohñ**tah*
- - Qual é o número do seu quarto?
  *kwal e oo **noo**muroo doo **seh**oo **kwar**too*
- ○ Vinte e cinco.
  *veent ee **seeñ**koo*
- - São cento e sessenta e cinco euros. Como vai pagar?
  *sãhoo **sehn**too ee su**sehn**tah ee **seeñ**koo e**roosh**. **koh**moo vaee pah**gar***
- ○ Com cartão de crédito.
  *kohm̃ kahr**tahoo** du **kre**deetoo*

Q How much is your hotel bill?

47

campsites

you may say ...

Have you got space for ...	Tem lugar para ...	*taheem loogar pahrah*
a car?	um carro?	*oom karroo*
a caravan?	uma caravana?	*oomah kahrahvahnah*
a tent?	uma tenda?	*oomah tehndah*
How much does it cost per day?	Qual é o preço por dia?	*kwal e oo prehsoo pohr deeah*
Where are ...	Onde são ...	*ohnd sãhoo*
the showers?	os duches?	*oosh dooshush*
the toilets	as casas de banho?	*ahsh kazahs du bahñnyoo*
the dustbins?	os caixotes do lixo?	*oosh kaishotush du leeshoo*
Is there	Há ...	*a*
a laundry	lavandaria?	*lahvahndahreeah*
a shop	loja?	*lojah*
a swimming pool?	piscina?	*peeshseenah*

you may hear ...

Temos um lugar livre para três noites.	*tehmoosh oom loogar leevru pahrah trehsh noheetush*	We have a pitch free for three nights.

48

check out 4

You have just arrived at the campsite.

○ Tem lugar para um carro e uma caravana?
taheem loogar pahrah oom karroo ee oomah kahra vahnah

- Temos.
tehmoosh

○ Qual é o preço?
kwal e oo prehsoo

- São três euros e cinquenta por dia para um carro e seis para uma caravana.
sãhoo trehsh eroosh ee seeñkwehñtahpoor deeah pahrah oom karroo ee saheesh pahrah oomah kahrahvahnah

(temos = yes, we have)

Q How much is the daily charge for the caravan?

self-catering & hostels

you may say ...

I've rented a villa.	Aluguei uma casa.	*ahloogahee oomah kazah*
How does ... work?	Como funciona ...	*kohmoo foonseeohnah*
the heating	o aquecimento?	*oo ahkeseemehntoo*
water	a água?	*ah agooah*
When are the dustbins emptied?	Quando é a recolha de lixo?	*kwahñdoo e ah rukohllah du leeshoo*
What time do you lock up?	A que horas fecham?	*a ku orosh fehshahm*
Can I hire ...	Posso alugar ...	*posoo aloogar*
sheets?	lençóis?	*lehnsoeesh*
a sleeping bag?	um saco-cama?	*oom sakoh-kahmah*

49

ch sounds like 'sh' in 'she':
duche *doosh*
chamo-me *shahmoomu*

nh sounds like 'ni' in 'onion':
banho *bahñnyoo*
dinheiro *deennyaheeroo*

try it out

lost for words

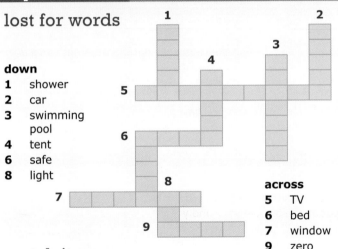

down
1 shower
2 car
3 swimming pool
4 tent
6 safe
8 light

across
5 TV
6 bed
7 window
9 zero

match it up

Match up the sentences on the left – all things you might say in a hotel – with the responses on the right.

1 Tem um quarto duplo?
2 O duche não funciona.
3 Como vai pagar?
4 Onde é o bar?
5 A que horas é o pequeno almoço?

a Mando alguém.
b Com cartão de crédito.
c Das oito às dez e meia.
d Lamento, o hotel está cheio.
e É ao lado do restaurante.

in the mix

See if you can unravel these words. The hints – all phrases you might say or hear in a hotel – should help you, but they are not in the right order!

1 tenio
2 apeasports
3 revelado
4 pramlobe
5 sadlout

Hints:
a Your room's on the sixth floor, so you get the ...
b I'd like a room for two ... and one child.
c There's a ... with the shower in my room.
d I want to stay for one ...
e Would you mind letting me have your ... please?

as if you were there

It's time to go home, and you're settling your hotel bill. Follow the prompts to play your part.

(Say you'd like to pay the bill)
Qual é o número do seu quarto, se faz favor?
(Say it's eight)
Ah, sim ... Como vai pagar?
(Ask him how much it is)
São sessenta e sete euros.
(Tell him in cash)
Muito bem.

linkup

Tem um quarto duplo?	**Do you have** a double room?
Há um elevador?	**Is there** a lift?
Onde é o restaurante?	**Where's** the restaurant?
É no primeiro andar.	**It's** on the first floor.
Não há ar condicionado.	**There isn't any** air conditioning.
A televisão **não funciona**.	The television **is not working**.

words for 'the' & 'a'

You've probably noticed that you say:
a cidade (the city) but **o** restaurante (the restaurant)
um quarto (a room) but **uma** planta (a map).
This is because in Portuguese words for nouns (things, places, people) are either masculine or feminine.

The word for 'the' is **o** for a singular masculine word and **a** for a singular feminine word.

The word for 'a' or 'an' is **um** for a masculine word and **uma** for a feminine word.

Generally, words ending in **o** are masculine and words ending in **a** are feminine.

The word for 'the' changes when you are talking about more than one thing – see the Language Builder, p129. ·····⟩

describing things

When you say 'The hotel is very big' in Portuguese, the words come in the same order as in English: O hotel é muito grande. But if you say 'a big hotel', the word order changes: um hotel grande.

Some more examples:
uma cama individual a single bed
um quarto duplo a double room

One or two exceptions to this practice:
o primeiro piso the first floor
o segundo prato the second course

The words grande, individual and duplo are known as adjectives or describing words.

Many adjectives in Portuguese end in **-o** or **-a**. Just as the words for 'a' and 'the' change according to the gender of the word they describe, so too do adjectives ending in **-o** or **-a**:

um hotel moderno a modern hotel (hotel is masculine)
uma igreja moderna a modern church (igreja is feminine)

Adjectives ending in **-e** and **-l** are the same for both masculine and feminine words:
um hotel grande a large hotel
uma cama grande a large bed
um tapete azul a blue carpet
uma toalha azul a blue towel

For more on using adjectives, see the Language Builder, pp130-131. ·····>

saying 'no': negatives

The word não means 'no':
Tem quartos vagos? – Não, lamento. Do you have rooms free? – No, sorry.
But it also means 'not', 'isn't' or 'doesn't':
Não há ar condicionado. There isn't any air conditioning.
O chuveiro não funciona. The shower doesn't work.

For more on negatives, see the Language Builder, p136. ·····>

Buying **Things**

opening hours

Shops are generally open Monday to Friday from 9am-1pm and 3pm-7pm, and Saturday morning. Shopping centres are open seven days a week from 10am to midnight. Larger shops and supermarkets accept credit cards. If you pay in cash, don't be surprised if the change is rounded up (or down) to the nearest five cents.

crafts

For traditional Portuguese souvenirs, try shops in the older neighbourhoods.

Ceramics Portuguese ceramics and **azulejos** (tiles) are distinctive and decorative. Popular styles include Barcelos pottery, brown with yellow spots, the intricate animal motifs of the Coimbra region and earthenware from Estremoz in the Alentejo and Caldas da Rainha in Estremadura.

Leather Albufeira in the Algarve has good-quality leather goods, while Madeira specializes in well-crafted footwear.

Metalwork Go to Silves, Portimão or Loulé in the Algarve to buy the **cataplana** cooking pots from its metal workshops.

Lace Hand-made lace is produced in Loulé, Olhão and Castro Marim in the Algarve.

Embroidery and bedspreads Visit the Beira Baixa, especially Castelo Branco, famed for its silk bedspreads, or Madeira, well known for its embroidery.

Tapestries Go to the inland Alentejo, especially at Portalegre where some spectacular tapestries sell for hundreds of pounds; or to Madeira where tapestry is an ancient art.

Carpets Also in the Alentejo, visit Arraiolos, a small town north of Évora, the centre for some beautiful brightly coloured Persian-influenced carpets.

Wickerwork and cork Baskets and mats are two finely crafted products from the Alentejo; wickerwork is also common in the Algarve and is the main trade in Camacha, in Madeira.

▮ markets

Most Portuguese towns have a weekly market, when people from the area congregate to buy and sell goods from livestock and clothes to crafts and local produce. They are well worth a visit just for the atmosphere.

Carcavelos Halfway along the Lisbon to Cascais train line, this Thursday market is a huge, sprawling event.

Feira da Ladra Lisbon's Tuesday and Saturday flea market, full of quirky cast-offs.

Barcelos Portugal's biggest market, held every Thursday, when its central square is crammed with everything from clothes to live chickens.

Many Barcelos stallholders rotate to weekly markets in other Minho towns, e.g. Fridays in Viana do Castelo, Wednesdays in Valença.

Elvas A Monday market when this cultured Alentejan town takes on an animated rural hue.

Portimão A vibrant flea-market takes place in this Algarve town on the first Sunday each month.

Alto Minho Don't miss these handicraft markets in Northern Portugal, where you can watch experts use traditional techniques to make a range of fine crafts. Any goods you buy will be certified by a Seal of Guarantee.

buying food ▮

If you're self-catering, or for a lunchtime picnic, the best place to buy supplies is from the town market; go early to get the best buys. Prices should be displayed and it's not usual to bargain.

You may want to take home:

Port and wine Port is excellent value and Portuguese wines are growing in reputation. Unless you happen to be passing a wine co-operative or want top-quality stuff, your best bet is to stock up on these at supermarkets, which tend to be cheaper than Porto's port lodges.

Olive oil This can be good value, either from supermarkets or from shops in the Alentejo or the Algarve where many of Portugal's olive groves are found.

phrasemaker

phrases to use anywhere
you may say ...

I'd like ...	Queria ...	*kureeah*
Do you have any ...	Tem ...	*taheem*
cheese?	queijo?	*kaheejoo*
jeans?	jeans?	*jeens*
Are there any ...	Há ...	*a*
bananas?	bananas?	*bahnahnahsh*
figs?	figos?	*feegoosh*
How much is that (altogether)?	Quanto é (tudo) isso?	*kwahñtoo e (toodoo) eesoo*
How much ...	Quanto ...	*kwahñtoo*
are they?	são?	*sãhoo*
does it cost?	custa?	*kooshtah*
do they cost?	custam?	*kooshtahm*
A ... please.	Um/Uma ..., se faz favor/por favor.	*oom/oomah ... su fash fahvohr/ poor favohr*
this one	este/esta	*ehsht/ehshtah*
that one	aquele/aquela	*ahkehl/ahkehlah*
That's all, thanks.	Mais nada, obrigado/a.	*maeesh nadah, obreegadoo/ah*
Can I pay ...	Posso pagar ...	*posoo pahgar*
with traveller's cheques?	com traveller's cheques?	*kohm travulahrsh shekush*
by credit card?	com cartão de crédito?	*kohm kahrtãhoo du kredeetoo*

you may hear ...

Que deseja?	*ku duzaheejah*	What can I do for you?
Posso ajudá-lo/la?	*posoo ahjooda-loo/lah*	Can I help you?
Lamento, não temos.	*lahmehntoo nãhoo tehmoosh*	I'm sorry, we have none (left).
Aqui tem.	*ahkee taheem*	Here you are.

Mais alguma coisa?	*maeesh al**goo**mah **kohee**zah*	**Anything else?**
É só?	*e so*	**Is that all?**
São … (euros) no total.	*sãhoo … (eroosh) noo too**tal***	**That's … (euros) altogether.**
Pague na caixa.	*pag nah **kaee**shah*	**Pay at the cash desk.**

shops

antique shop	o antiquário	*oo ahnteekoo**oa**reeoo*
bread shop	a padaria	*ah padah**ree**ah*
butcher's	o talho	*oo **ta**llo*
cake/pastry shop	a pastelaria	*ah pashtulah**ree**ah*
clothes shop	a loja de roupas	*ah **lo**jah du **roh**pahsh*
department store	o grande armazém	*oo grand armah**zaheem̃***
fishmonger's	a peixaria	*ah paheeshah**ree**ah*
food shop/grocer's	a mercearia	*ah murseeah**ree**ah*
health food shop	a loja de produtos dietéticos	*ah **lo**jah du proo**doo**toosh deeu**te**teekoosh*
jeweller's	a joalharia	*ah jooahllah**ree**ah*
laundry (dry cleaner's)	a lavandaria (a seco)	*ah lahvahndah**ree**ah (ah **seh**koo)*
market	o mercado	*oo mur**ka**doo*
newsagent's kiosk	o quiosque de jornais	*oo kee**oshk** du joor**naee**sh*
photography shop	a loja de artigos fotográficos	*ah **lo**jah du ahr**tee**goosh footoo**gra**feekoosh*
shoe shop	a sapataria	*ah sahpahtah**ree**ah*
shopping centre	o centro comercial	*oo **sehñ**troo koomursee**al***
supermarket	o supermercado	*oo soopermur**ka**doo*
tobacconist's	a tabacaria	*ah tahbahkah**ree**ah*
wine merchant's	o comerciante de vinhos	*oo koomursee**ahnt** du **veeñ**nyoosh*

food shopping

you may say ...

How much is a kilo of ...
  oranges?
	Quanto é o quilo de ...
	  laranjas?
		kwahñto e oo keeloo du
		  lahrahñjahsh

a kilo of ...
  apples
  potatoes
	um quilo de ...
	  maçãs
	  batatas
		ooñ keeloo du
		  mahsahñsh
		  bahtatahsh

half a kilo of ...
  cheese
  cherries
	meio quilo de ...
	  queijo
	  cerejas
		maheeoo keeloo du
		  kaheejoo
		  suraheejahsh

100 grammes of ...
  smoked ham
  sweets
(See numbers, p14)
	cem gramas de
	  presunto
	  rebuçados
		sehñ grahmahsh du
		  pruzooñtoo
		  rruboosadoosh

a bottle/tin of ...	uma garrafa/lata de ...	*oomah gahrrafah/latah du*
a jar/packet/sachet of ...	um frasco/pacote/pacotinho de ...	*ooñ frashkoo/pahkot/pahkooteennyoo du*
a slice/three slices of ...	uma fatia/três fatias de ...	*oomah fahteeah/trêhsh fahteeahsh du*
Can I try (some/a piece)?	Posso provar?	*posoo proovar*
A bit more/less, please.	Um bocado mais/menos, se faz favor.	*ooñ bookadoo maheesh/mehnoosh su fash fahvohr*

Quanto/a quer?	*kwahñtolah ker*	How much would you like?
Quantos/as?	*kwahñtoosh/ahsh*	How many?
Qual (prefere)?	*kwal (prehfehreh)*	Which one (do you prefer)?
Temos vários tipos.	*tehmoosh vareeoosh teepoosh*	We have several types.

fruit & nuts

almonds	as amêndoas	*ahsh ahmehndooahsh*
apples	as maçãs	*ahsh mahsānsh*
apricots	os alperces	*oosh alpersush*
bananas	as bananas	*ahsh bahnahnahsh*
blackberries	as amoras	*ahsh ahmorahsh*
chestnuts	as castanhas	*ahsh kahshtahñnyahsh*
figs	os figos	*oosh feegoos*
grapefruit	a toranja	*ah toorahñjah*
grapes	as uvas	*ahsh oovahsh*
hazelnuts	as avelãs	*ahsh ahvulāhsh*
lemons	os limões	*oosh leemōheesh*
melon	o melão	*oo mulāhoo*
oranges	as laranjas	*ahsh lahrahñjahsh*
peaches	os pêssegos	*oosh pehsugoosh*
peanuts	os amendoins	*oosh ahmehndooeeñsh*
pears	as pêras	*ahsh pehrahsh*
pineapple	o ananás	*oo ahnahnash*
plums	as ameixas	*ahsh ahmaheeshahsh*
raspberries	as framboesas	*ahsh frahmbooehzahsh*
strawberries	os morangos	*oosh moorahñgoosh*
walnuts	as nozes	*ahsh nozush*
watermelon	a melancia	*ah mulahnseeah*

vegetables

aubergine	a berinjela	*ah buren**je**lah*
green beans	os feijões verdes	*oosh fahee**jõheensh vehr**dush*
carrots	as cenouras	*ahsh su**noh**rahsh*
cucumber	o pepino	*oo pup**een**oo*
garlic	o alho	*oo **a**lloo*
lentils	as lentilhas	*ahsh lehn**tee**llash*
lettuce	a alface	*ah al**fa**su*
mushrooms	os cogumelos	*oosh koogoo**me**loosh*
onions	as cebolas	*ahsh su**boh**lahsh*
peas	as ervilhas	*ahsh ehr**vee**llahsh*
peppers	os pimentos	*oosh pee**mehñ**toosh*
potatoes	as batatas	*ahsh bah**ta**tahsh*
radishes	os rabanetes	*oosh rrahbah**neh**tush*
spinach	o(s) espinafre(s)	*oo(sh) eeshpee**na**fru(sh)*
sweetcorn	o milho	*oo **mee**lloo*
tomatoes	os tomates	*oosh too**ma**tush*

check out 1

You want to buy some smoked ham and cheese.

- ○ Bom dia, queria meio quilo de presunto, se faz favor.
  bohm deeah kureeah maheeoo keeloo du pruzoontoo su fash fahvohr
- - Com certeza. Mais alguma coisa?
  kohm surtehzah. maeesh algoomah koheezah
- ○ Duzentos gramas de queijo.
  doozehntohsh grahmahsh du kaheejoo

  (com certeza = certainly)

Q How much cheese do you buy?

supermarket

bread	o pão	*oo pãhoo*
bread rolls	os papos-secos/ pãezinhos	*oosh papoosh sehkoosh/ pãheenzeeñnyoosh*
cheesecakes	as queijadas	*ahsh kaheejadahsh*
boiled ham	o fiambre	*oo feeambru*
honey	o mel	*oo mel*
lemonade	a limonada	*ah leemoonadah*
milk	o leite	*oo laheet*
(sparkling/still) mineral water	a água mineral (com gás/sem gás)	*ah agooah meenural (kohm gash/saheem gash)*
spicy sausage	o chouriço	*oo shohreesoo*
washing powder	o detergente para roupa	*oo duturjehnt pahrah rrohoopah*
washing-up liquid	o detergente para louça	*oo duturjehnt pahrah lohoosa*

buying clothes
you may say ...

I'm just looking, thank you.	Estou só a ver, obrigado/a.	*eeshtoh so ah vehr obrigadoo/ah*
I'd like ...	Queria ...	*kureeah*
a shirt.	uma camisa.	*oomah kahmeezah*
a pair of trousers.	umas calças.	*oomahsh kalsahsh*
I'm size 40.	O meu número é quarenta.	*oo mehoo noomuroo e kwarehñtah*
Can I try it on?	Posso experimentá-lo/-la?	*posoo aheesh-preemehñta-loo/-lah*
Can I try them on?	Posso experimentá-los/-las?	*posoo aheesh-preemehñta-loosh/-lahsh*
They're a bit ...	São um bocado ...	*sãhoo oom bookadoo*
small.	pequenos/as.	*pukehnoosh/ahsh*
big.	grandes.	*grahndush*
They're too ...	São demasiado ...	*sãhoo dumahzeeadoo*
narrow.	estreitos/as.	*eeshtraheetoosh/ahsh*
wide.	largos/as.	*largoosh/ahsh*
Do you have the same in ...	Tem isso em ...	*taheem eesoo aheem*
green?	verde?	*vehrd*
silk?	seda?	*sehdah*
wool?	lã?	*lãm*
cotton?	algodão?	*algoodãhoo*

Do you have anything ...	Tem mais ...	*taheem maheesh*
smaller?	pequeno/a?	*pukehnoo/ah*
cheaper?	barato/a?	*bahratoo/ah*
I like (it/them).	Gosto.	**gosh**too
I don't like (it/them).	Não gosto.	*nãhoo* **gosh**too
It's very expensive.	É muito caro/a.	*e* **moohee**ñ*too* **ka**roo/ah
I'll take it.	Fico com ele/ela.	**fee**koo kohm ehl/**e**lah
I'll take them.	Fico com eles/elas.	**fee**koo kohm **eh**lush/**e**lahsh
I'll think about it.	Vou pensar.	*voh pehn**sar***

you may hear ...

Que número?	*ku **noo**muroo*	What size are you?
Em que cor?	*aheem ku cohr*	What colour?
O senhor/A senhora gosta ...	*oo sun**nyohr**/ah sun**nyoh**rah **gosh**tah*	How do you like ...
dele/dela?	*dehl/**de**lah*	it?
deles/delas?	**deh**lush/**de**lahsh	them?
Aquele/Aquela é maior.	*ah**kehl**/ah**ke**lah e mahee**or***	That one is bigger.

department store

you may say ...

Where is the ... department?	Onde é a secção de ...?	*ohnd e a sek**sãhoo** du*
Where are the checkouts?	Onde são as caixas?	*ohnd sãhoo ash **kaee**shash*
Is there a lift?	Há elevador?	*a eeluvah**dohr***
Where can I find ...	Onde posso encontrar ...	*ohnd **po**soo ehnkohntrar*
ladies'/men's fashion?	moda de senhoras/ homens?	***mo**dah du sun**nyoh**rahsh/ **oma**heensh*
beauty products?	produtos de beleza?	*proo**doo**toosh du bu**leh**zah*

check out 2

You want to buy a T-shirt.

○ Posso ajudá-lo?
*po*soo ahjoo*da*-loo

- Gosto desta T-shirt.
***gosh**too **desh**tah tee-**shahr**t*

○ Que número?
*ku **noo**muroo*

- O meu número é quarenta e um.
*oo **meh**oo **noo**muroo e kwah**rehñ**tah ee oom*

○ Esta é muito pequena. Aquela é maior.
esh**tah e **mooeeñ**too pu**keh**nah. ah**kel**ah e maee**or

- Posso prová-la?
*po*soo proo**va**-lah*

○ Pode. Venha por aqui, se faz favor.
*pod. **vaheeñ**nyah poor ah**kee** su fash fah**vohr***

(venha por aqui = come this way)

Q What size T-shirt do you ask for?
Are you able to try it on?

| no rés-do-chão | *noo rresh-doo-shãhoo* | **on the ground floor** |
| no primeiro/ segundo andar | *no preemaheeroo/ sugoondoo) ahndar* | **on the first/second floor** |

clothes & accessories

belt	o cinto	*oo seentoo*
coat	o casaco	*oo kahzakoo*
dress	o vestido	*oo vushteedoo*
gloves	as luvas	*ahsh loovahsh*
hat	o chapéu	*oo shahpeoo*
jacket	o casaco	*oo kahzakoo*
jeans	os jeans	*oosh jeens*
scarf	o cachecol	*oo kashkol*
shirt	a camisa	*ah kahmeezah*
shoes	os sapatos	*oosh sahpatoosh*
shorts	os calções	*oosh kalsõheensh*
skirt	a saia	*ah saeeah*
socks	as peúgas	*ahsh peeoogahsh*
sunglasses	os óculos de sol	*oosh okooloosh du sol*
sweater	a camisola	*ah kahmeezolah*
swimming costume	o fato de banho	*oo fatoo du bahñnyoo*
tie	a gravata	*ah grahvatah*
trousers	as calças	*ahsh kalsahsh*

buying stamps & newspapers

you may say ...

How much is a stamp for ...	Quanto é um selo para ...	*kwahñtoo e ooñ sehloo pahrah*
Great Britain?	a Grã-Bretanha?	*ah gran brehtãneeah*
the USA?	os Estados Unidos?	*oosh eeshtadoosh ooneedoosh*
for ...	para ...	*pahrah*
a letter	uma carta	*oomah kartah*
a postcard	um postal	*ooñ pooshtal*
I'd like to send this to Australia.	Queria mandar isto para Austrália.	*kureeah mahndar eeshtoo pahrah aooshtraleeah*
A telephone card, please.	Um cartão de telefone, se faz favor.	*ooñ kahrtão du tulufon su fash fahvohr*
Do you have ...	Tem ...	*taheeñ*
English newspapers?	jornais ingleses?	*joornaeesh eenglehzush*
a guidebook?	um guia?	*ooñ geeah*
a map of the city?	uma planta da cidade?	*oomah plahntah dah seedadu*

check out 3

You want to buy some stamps.

- ○ Vendem selos?
  vehñdaheeñ sehloosh
- – Vendemos sim. Quantos quer?
  vehndehmoosh seem. kwahñtoosh ker
- ○ Queria quatro selos para a Grã-Bretanha.
  kureeah kwatroo sehloosh pahrah a gran brehtãneeah
- – São três euros.
  sãhoo trehsh eroosh.

Q How much will you have to pay?

photography

you may say ...

Can you develop this?	Pode revelar isto?	*pod rruvular eeshtoo*
When will it be ready?	Quando estará pronto?	*kwahñdoo eeshtahra prohntoo*
Can you print from this memory card?	Pode imprimir deste cartão de memória?	*pod eempreemeer dehsht kahrtão du mumoreeah*
a 35-mm film	um rolo de trinta e cinco milímetros	*ooñ rohloo du treeñtah ee seeñkoo meeleemutroosh*
a black and white film	um filme a preto e branco	*ooñ feelm ah prehtoo ee brahñkoo*
a memory card	um cartão de memória	*ooñ kahrtãhoo du mumoreeah*
a disposable camera	uma máquina descartável	*oomah makeenah duskahrtavel*
batteries	as pilhas	*ahsh peellahsh*

you may hear ...

hoje/amanhã	*ohj/amahñnyãh*	today/tomorrow
daqui a ...	*dahkee ah*	in ...
uma hora	*oomah orah*	one hour
três horas	*trehsh orahsh*	three hours
serviço rápido	*surveesoo rrapeedoo*	express service
Que tamanho deseja as fotos?	*ku tahmahnnyoo dusaheejah ahsh fotoosh*	What size do you want your prints?
mate	*mat*	matt
brilhante	*breellahnt*	gloss

try it out

in the mix

See if you can unravel the words on this grocery shopping list. E.g. uma *taal* de *shandrais* – uma *lata* de *sardinhas*

1   cem *smagra* de *joique*
2   uma *farraga* de água *lermina*
3   meio *liquo* de *sounterp*
4   um *trilo* de *hinov*
5   um *houçocri*

opposites attract

Find the opposites for these words – all useful when out shopping.

1 grande   2 estreito   3 barato

as if you were there

You are trying on some shoes in a shoe shop. Follow the prompts to play your part.

(Say that you want to try on some shoes)
Com certeza. Qual é o seu número?
(Say that you are size 39)

After trying on several pairs, you decide which you like best.

(Say that you'll take them)

Buying **Things**

linkup

Tem figos?	**Do you have** any figs?
Vendem selos?	**Do you sell** stamps?
Queria meio quilo de presunto.	**I'd like** half a kilo of smoked ham.
Dê-me dois quilos.	**I'll have** two kilos.
Quanto é esta camisa?	**How much is** this shirt?

asking about availability

There are two main ways of asking this:
Tem figos? Do you have any figs?
Há bananas? Are there any bananas?

And the replies you are likely to hear are:
Sim, temos figos./Não, não temos figos. Yes, we have some figs./No, we don't have any figs.
Sim, há bananas./Não, não há bananas. Yes, we have (some) bananas./No, we don't have any bananas.

Notice that in Portuguese you don't need the word for 'some' or 'any'.

Note also that the useful word há means both 'Is there/are there?' and 'There is/there are'.
Há um banco perto daqui? Is there a bank near here?
Há um na esquina. There's one on the corner.

more than one

To talk about more than one of something in Portuguese, you usually just add **-s**:

duas camisas two shirts
cinco quilos five kilos

Some common exceptions are words ending in **-al** and **-ão**:

o postal, os postais postcard, postcards
o jornal, os jornais newspaper, newspapers
o limão, os limões lemon, lemons
o melão, os melões melon, melons

For more on plurals, see the Language Builder, pp129-130. ⋯⋯▷

Café **Life**

where to eat

Pastelarias are your best bet for breakfast and tea, usually offering a wide range of pastries, cakes, tea and coffee. Busy times are 7am-9am, and late afternoon. Don't miss **pastéis de nata** (custard tarts) traditionally from Belém: fresh and dusted with cinnamon, they make the perfect tea-time snack. Many **pastelarias** also offer lunch dishes such as **pastéis de bacalhau** (fishcakes), **pastéis de carne** (meat pies) and **sandes** (sandwiches).

Cafés offer a similar range of breakfast treats, or a lunch of soups, **tostas** (toasted sandwiches), **bifanas** or **pregos** (grilled pork or steak rolls). Larger cafés and **tascas** (taverns) serve full set lunches.

Cervejaria Large cafés serving beer and shellfish.

what to drink

Vinho do Porto is fortified wine, perhaps Portugal's most famous drink. Try a cool **porto branco** (white port) as an aperitif.

Vinho verde These light, young wines are extremely tasty and refreshing, though the white is more accessible than the red.

Vinho maduro Almost every region has a fine mature wine. Some of the best are Dão, Douro, Bairrada, and Colares.

Moscatel A sweet, fruity dessert wine from just south of Lisbon.

Madeira Cool fortified wine; try the sweet Malmsey and Bual, the medium Verdelho or the dry Sercial.

Macieira One of the smoothest of Portugal's potent **aguardentes** (brandies), a good drink to round off a meal.

Ginginha A cherry liqueur, which is served with or without the stone.

Bica A wickedly strong espresso coffee, guaranteed to perk you up in the mornings.

Chá com limão Tea with lemon, a refreshing drink best had in one of Portugal's many **salões de chá** (tea rooms).

phrasemaker

asking what there is
you may say ...

Do you have ...	Tem ...	*taheem̃*
sandwiches?	sandes?	***sahn**dush*
beer?	cerveja?	*sur**vahee**jah*
What ... do you have?	Que ... tem?	*ku ... taheem̃*
cakes	bolos	***boh**loosh*
snacks	refeições leves	*rrufahee**sõeesh** **le**vush*
flavours	sabores	*sah**boh**rush*
Do you have any soft drinks, please?	Há refrigerantes, se faz favor?	*a rrufreeju**rahn**tush su fash fah**vohr***
Can I see what you have?	Pode-se ver o que tem?	***po**dusu vehr oo ku taheem̃*
What do you recommend?	O que recomenda?	*oo ku rrukoo**mehn**dah*

you may hear ...

Posso ajudá-lo/la?	***po**soo ahjoo**da**-loo/lah*	Can I help you?
O que deseja comer/beber?	*oo ku du**zahee**jah koo**mehr**/bu**behr***	What would you like to eat/drink?
Lamento, não temos.	*lah**mehn**too nãhoo **teh**moosh*	I'm sorry, we haven't any.

72

Só temos ...	*so **teh**moosh*	We only have ...
Tem ...	*taheem*	We have ...
chocolate.	*shookoolat*	chocolate.
alperce.	*al**pers***	apricot.
café.	*kah**fe***	coffee.
pistacho.	*pis**tash**oo*	pistachio.
morango.	*moo**rahn**goo*	strawberry.
baunilha.	*baoo**nee**llah*	vanilla.

check out 1
You want a lunchtime snack.

- O que deseja?
  *oo ku du**zahee**jah*
- Tem sandes?
  *taheem **sahn**dush*
- Lamento, não temos.
  *lah**mehn**too nãhoo **teh**moosh*

Q Do they have any sandwiches?

ordering
you may say ...

I'd like ...	Queria ...	*ku**ree**ah*
a milky coffee.	um galão.	*oom gah**lãh**oo*
breakfast.	o pequeno almoço.	*oo pu**keh**noo al**moh**soo*
an ice cream.	um gelado.	*oom ju**la**doo*
I'll take this.	Quero isto.	*keroo **eesh**too*
I'd like to try ...	Queria provar ...	*ku**ree**ah proo**var***
Bring me ...	Traga-me ...	*tra**gah**mu*
a ham and cheese toasted sandwich.	uma tosta mista.	*oomah **tosh**tah **meesh**tah*

For me ...
  a ham sandwich.
	Para mim ...
	  uma sandes de
	  fiambre.
		pahrah meeñ
		  *oomah **sahn**dush du*
		  feeambru

some toast.	uma torrada.	*oomah toorradah*

a portion of ...
  chips
	uma dose de ...
	  batatas fritas
		oomah doz du
		  *bahtatahsh **free**tahsh*

Waiter! Another beer!	Faz favor! Mais uma cerveja!	*fash fah**vohr*** *maheesh **oo**mah* *survaheejah*
a bottle/carafe/glass of ...	uma garrafa/um jarro/um copo de ...	*oomah gah**rra**fah/oom **ja**rroo/oom **ko**poo du*
How much is it, please?	Quanto é, se faz favor?	*kwahñtoo e su fash* *fah**vohr***

you may hear ...

Grande ou pequeno/ a?	*grahnd oh pu**keh**noo/ah*	Large or small?
Fresco/a ou natural?	*frehshkoo oh/ah nahtoo**ral***	Ice cold or room temperature?
Com gelo?	*kohñ **jeh**loo*	With ice?
Mais alguma coisa?	*maheesh alg**oo**mah **koh**eezah*	Anything else?
É só?	*e so*	Is that all?
Que sabor?	*ku sah**bohr***	Which flavour?
Qual?	*kwal*	Which one?
Aqui está.	*ah**kee** ee**sh**ta*	Here you are.
Em seguida.	*eñ su**gee**du*	Straight away.
É self-service.	*e self-service*	It's self-service.
O pré-pagamento.	*oo pre-pahgah**mehn**too*	Payment in advance.
Tem troco?	*taheeñ **troh**koo*	Do you have change?
Não tem de quê.	*nähoo taheeñ du keh*	You're welcome.

Café **Life**

soft drinks

cola	uma cola	*oomah kolah*
... juice	um sumo de ...	*oom soomoo du*
fruit	fruta	*frootah*
orange	laranja	*lahrahnjah*
pineapple	ananás	*ahnahnash*
grape	uva	*oovah*
peach	pêssego	*pehsugoo*
lemonade	uma limonada	*oomah leemoonadah*
milk	um leite	*oom laheet*
milkshake	um batido	*oom bahteedoo*
... (mineral) water	uma água (mineral) ...	*oomah agooah (meenural)*
sparkling	com gás	*kohm gash*
still	sem gás	*saheem gash*
ice cold	fresca	*frehshkah*
room temperature	natural	*nahtooral*
orangeade	uma laranjada	*oomah lahrahnjadah*

alcoholic drinks

beer/lager	uma cerveja	*oomah survaheejah*
beer, draught	uma imperial/uma caneca/o fino (in the north)	*oomah eempureeal/ oomah kahnekah/oom feenoo*
beer, bottled	uma garrafa de cerveja	*oomah gahrrafah du survaheejah*
brandy	uma aguardente	*oomah agooahrdehnt*
cognac	um conhaque	*oom konnyak*
gin and tonic	um gin-tónico	*oom jeentoneekoo*
port	um vinho do Porto	*oom veeñnyoo doo pohrtoo*
rum	um rum	*oom room*
sherry	um vinho xerez	*oom veennyoo shurehsh*
whisky	um uísque	*oom ooeeshk*
red/white/rosé wine	um vinho tinto/ branco/rosado	*oom veeñnyoo teentoo /brahñkoo/rrozadoo*
dry/sweet	seco/doce	*sehkoo/dohs*

check out 2

You missed breakfast at the hotel and go to a café.

○ Tem pequeno almoço?
taheem pukehnoo almohsoo

- Sim, senhora. Temos bolos e torradas, se faz favor.
seem sunnyhohrah. tehmoosh bohloosh ee toorradahsh su fash fahvohr

○ Uma torrada, se faz favor.
oomah toorradah su fash fahvohr

- O que deseja beber?
oo ku duzaheejah bubehr

Q   What does the waiter ask you?

hot drinks

black coffee (very strong)	uma bica/um café	*oomah beekah/oom kahfe*
coffee	um café	*oom kahfe*
decaffeinated coffee	um café descafeinado	*oom kahfe dushkahfaheenadoo*
hot chocolate	um chocolate quente	*oom shookoolat kehnt*
tea	um chá	*oom sha*
with milk/lemon	com leite/limão	*kohm laheet/ leemãhoo*
white coffee	um café com leite/ um garoto	*oom kahfe kohm laheet/oo gahrohtoo*
large, milky coffee (served in a glass)	um galão	*oom gahlãhoo*

typical snacks

os acepipes variados	*oosh ahsupeepush vahreeadoosh*	assorted appetizers (hors-d'œuvres)
as azeitonas (recheadas)	*ahsh ahzaheetohnahsh (rusheeadahsh)*	(stuffed) olives
os bolinhos de amêndoa	*oosh booleeññyoosh du ahmehndooah*	almond biscuits
o bolo	*oo bohloo*	cake
os camarões	*oosh kahmahrōeensh*	shrimp
as carnes frias	*ahsh karnush freeahsh*	cold meats
o chouriço	*oo shouhreesoo*	spicy sausage
as lulas grelhadas	*ahsh loolahsh grullladahsh*	grilled squid
os pastéis de ... bacalhau carne peixe	*oosh pahshtaheesh du bahkahllaoo paheesh karn*	... pasties salted cod meat fish
o pastel de nata/ de Belém	*oo pahshtel du natah/du behlem̃*	custard tart
a queijada	*ah kaheejadah*	cheese tart
os rissóis	*oosh rreesoeesh*	fried filled pasties
as sardinhas	*ahsh sahrdeeññyahsh*	sardines

check out 3

You stop for a refreshing ice cream.

- ○ Um gelado de morango, se faz favor.
  oom juladoo du moorahngoo su fash fahvohr

- Ah, lamento. Só temos de baunilha.
  ah lahmehntoo. so tehmoosh du baooneellah

Q What flavour are you offered?

77

sound check

If it's not stressed, **e** sounds like the 'a' in 'across'. If it is stressed, it sounds like 'eh' or 'e' in 'belt':
pequeno *pukehnoo*

If it's before an **i**, the **e** and **i** together make the sound 'ay', and at the end of a word it's often not pronounced:
leite *laheet*

Before **m** it makes the nasal sound:
tem *taheem̃* (said through the nose).

At the beginning of a word it sounds like 'i' in 'hit':
está *eeshta*

é sounds like 'eh' or 'e' in 'egg': café *kahfe*

ê sounds like 'a' in 'hay': você *voseh*

try it out

in the mix
Use the clue to unravel these snacks and drinks.

1 cold breakfast drink ed mosu atfru
2 sounds cold, but refreshing retegeranfri
3 icy dessert ladoge
4 milky drink tidoba
5 more than just a piece of bread toast
6 breakfast cup rotoga
7 beefy snack gopre
8 fruit of the summer mogoran
9 lunchtime snack dessan

Café **Life**

downword

Fill in the items going down and you'll be able to work out the edible treat across the top.

1 Popular ice cream flavour.
2 Nearly always in your pocket or purse.
3 Have we? Yes, we have!
4 Opposite of com.
5 Those tasty filled pasties.
6 A complement to gin. Sounds good for you!
7 Strawberry, vanilla and pistachio are all ... of ice cream.

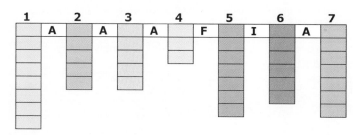

as if you were there

You want to order aperitifs in a bar. Follow the prompts to play your part.

(Ask for a gin and tonic)
Com gelo?
(Say yes, and order a white wine as well)
Mais alguma coisa? Azeitonas?
(Say you want some assorted appetizers)
Em seguida, senhor.

linkup

key phrases

Tem gelados?	**Do you have** ice creams?
Há pastéis de bacalhau?	**Are there** salted cod pasties?
Dê-me uma tosta mista.	**I'll have** a toasted cheese and ham sandwich.
Que refrigerantes **tem**?	**What** cool soft drinks **do you have**?
Para mim, uma cerveja.	A beer **for me**.

requesting things

The easiest way to order food or drink is simply to say what you want:

Duas cervejas, se faz favor. Two beers, please.

You can also say:

Para mim, uma cerveja. A beer for me.

or:

Dê-me uma tosta mista.

Traga-me uma bica.

Both these are equivalent to the English 'Please could I have ...', or Give me ...'.

Another option is:

Pode trazer-me mais pão? Can you bring me more bread?

Or the more formal:

Podia trazer-me mais pão? Could you bring me more bread?

Eating **Out**

meal times

The Portuguese enjoy eating out and do so frequently. Lunchtime **pratos do dia** (specials) are very reasonable, and most restaurants will be packed during office lunch breaks (around noon-3pm). Restaurant meals during evenings (around 7pm-10pm, later in summer resorts) and at weekends are slightly more expensive, although the **ementa turística** (set meal of the day) is always good value. Restaurant meals tend to be family affairs; don't be surprised to see children out and about until midnight.

where to eat

Restaurants are your best bet for a full evening meal, along with **cervejarias** (large places often selling seafood and beers) or **churrascarias** (specializing in grilled or barbecued food). **Marisqueiras** (specialising in seafood) tend to be marginally more expensive.

Cafés see p71.

Fast food Large towns and resorts now have a growing number of fast-food chains, which tend to be more expensive than dishes at local restaurants.

Vegetarian options Vegetarians have a hard time in most restaurants and may be limited to starter or side options such as vegetable soup, omelette or salads.

types of food

Being an Atlantic country, fish and seafood are usually of a high standard in Portugal. Most restaurants will have a local fresh fish, **bacalhau** (salted cod) or seafood dish, whilst pork and chicken are reliable staples for meat-eaters. Beef, lamb, goat, rabbit, suckling pig and even wild boar are also fairly common. Portuguese food tends to be cooked with plenty of olive oil, garlic and coriander, although sauces and accompanying vegetables are a rare feature.

If you are in the region, try these local specialities:

Porto and the Douro Tripas à moda do Porto (tripe with beans); cação em vinho tinto (a thick fish stew in a red wine sauce).

Minho Lombo de porco assado (roast pork loin); fatias de Braga (a sweet almond cake).

Trás-os-Montes Sopa de castanha (chestnut soup); feijoada (meat and bean stew); nogado (nut and honey nougat).

Beira Alta Queijo da serra (a mountain cheese); chouriço (a spicy sausage); fios (a Moorish sweetmeat, meaning 'threads').

Beira Baixa Cabrito assado (roast kid).

Coimbra and Beira Litoral Sopa de caldeirada (mixed fish soup); leitão assado (roast suckling pig).

Lisbon and Estremadura Lulas fritas (fried fresh squid); iscas (marinated liver cooked with presunto and potatoes); santola recheada (stuffed spider crab).

Ribatejo Favas à ribatejana (broad bean and pork stew); pudim de cenouras (carrot pudding).

Alentejo Açorda (a white sauce to accompany other dishes); lulas recheadas (stuffed squid); cerieaia com ameixas (sponge cake with plum sauce), cheeses from Nisa.

Algarve Sardinhas no churrasco (barbecued sardines); cataplana de amêijoas (clam stew); brandymel (a honey-brandy).

Madeira Bife de atum e milho frito (tuna steaks with fried maize); bolo de mel (honey cake); maracujá (passionfruit juice).

phrasemaker

finding somewhere to eat

you may say ...

Is there a good restaurant near here?	Há um bom restaurante perto daqui?	*a oom bohm rushtaoorahnt pertoo dahkee*
I'd like to book a table for ... two people. tonight at 8pm. (See days, p17 and times, p14)	Queria reservar uma mesa para ... duas pessoas. hoje às oito horas.	*kureeah rruzurvahr oomah mehzah pahrah dooahs pusohahss ohj a oheetoh orahss*
I have a table booked for three.	Tenho uma mesa reservada para três pessoas.	*tañnyoo oomah mehzah rruzurvadah pahrah trehsh pusohahss*
It's in the name of ...	Está em nome de ...	*eeshta ehm nohmu du*
Do you have a table now?	Tem uma mesa agora?	*taheem oomah mehzah ahgorah*
Can we eat ... outside? near the window? away from the door? in a non-smoking area?	Pode-se comer ... lá fora? perto da janela? longe da porta? numa zona para não fumadores?	*podsu koomehr la forah pertoo dah jahnelah lohnj dah portah noomah zohnah pahrah nãhoo foomahdohrush*

you may hear ...

| Queria sentar-se aqui? | *kureeah shentarsu ahkee* | Would you like to sit here? |
| Queria tomar ... uma bebida? um aperitivo? | *kureeah toomar oomah bubeedah ooñ ahpureeteevoo* | Would you like ... a drink? an aperitif? |

check out 1

You ask for a table in a busy restaurant.

○ Tem uma mesa para quatro pessoas?
taheeñ oomah mehzah pahrah kwatroo pusohahsh

- Podem esperar uns dez minutos?
podeeñ eehspurar ooñsh desh meenootoosh

○ Sim. Pode-se comer lá fora?
seeñ. podsu koomehr la forah

- Lamento, não temos mesa lá fora. Queriam sentar-se perto da janela?
lahmehntoo nãhoo tehmoosh mehzah la forah. kureeahñ shentarsu pertoo dah jahnelah

How long do you have to wait for?
You get a table outside: true or false?

asking about the menu

you may say ...

The menu, please.	A ementa, se faz favor.	*ah eemehntah su fash fahvohr*
Have you got a set menu?	Tem ementa turística?	*taheeñ eemehntah tooreeshteekah*
Does that include ... bread? wine?	Inclui ... pão? vinho?	*eenklooee pãhoo veennyo*
What is the dish of the day?	Qual é o prato do dia?	*kwal e oo pratoo ku deeah*
What do you recommend?	O que recomenda?	*oo ku rrukoomehndah*

What's the local speciality?	Qual é a especialidade da região?	*kwal e ah eehspuseeahleedad dah rrugeeãhoo*
Can you tell me what ... is?	Pode dizer-me o que é ...?	*pod deezehrmu oo ku e*
I can't eat ...	Não posso comer ...	*nãhoo posoo koomehr*
What is in the sauce?	Como é o molho?	*kohmoo e oo mohlloo*
I'm allergic to ... dairy products.	Sou alérgico/a a ... produtos lácteos.	*soh ahlerjeekoo/ah ah proodootoosh lakteeoosh*
I'm ... vegetarian. vegan.	Sou ... vegetariano/a. vegetalista.	*soh vujutahrreahnoo/ah vuhjutahleeshtah*
Does it contain ... nuts? wheat?	Contém ... nozes? trigo?	*kohntaheeñ nozeesh treegoo*

you may hear ...

Hoje temos ...	*ohj tehmoosh*	Today we have ...
Recomendamos ...	*rrukoomehndahmoosh*	We recommend ...
Lamento, só temos ...	*lahmehntoo so tehmoosh*	I'm sorry, we only have ...
É ... um peixe grande e branco. um tipo de cebola.	*e ooñ paheesh grahnd ee brahnkoo ooñ teepoo du subohlah*	It's ... a large white fish. a kind of onion.

ordering

you may say ...

I'll have ... for the first course.	Queria ... para o primeiro prato.	kureeah ... pahrah oo preemaheeroo prato
the main course. dessert.	o prato principal. a sobremesa.	oo prato preenseepal ah soobrumehzah
I'd like a half-portion of ...	Queria meia dose de ...	kureeah maheeah doz du
rare	mal passado/a	mal pahsadoo/ah
medium	no ponto	noo pontu
well done	bem passado/a	behm pahsadoo/ah

you may hear ...

Queria pedir agora?	kureeah pudeer ahgorah	Would you like to order now?
O que deseja?	oo ku duzaheejah	What would you like?
Para beber?	pahrah bubehr	To drink?
Quer sobremesa?	ker soobrumehzah	Would you like dessert?
Como deseja a carne?	kohmoo duzaheejah ah karn	How would you like your meat?

check out 2

You make enquiries about the dish of the day.

○ Qual é o prato do dia?
 kwal e oo prato doo deeah

- Frango com batatas fritas.
 frahngoo kohm bahtatahs freetahs

○ Inclui vinho?
 eenklooee veennyoo

- Sim, inclui uma garrafa de vinho.
 seem eenklooee oomah gahrrafah du veennyoo

Q   What is the dish of the day: fish, chicken, veal or pork?
     What is included with the meal?

drinks

you may say ...

Is there a wine list?	Há uma lista dos vinhos?	*a oomah leeshtah doosh veennyosh*
a bottle/half-bottle of ...	uma garrafa/meia garrafa de ...	*oomah gahrrafah/ maheeah gahrrafah du*
... wine red white rosé	vinho ... tinto branco rosado	*veennyo teentoo brahñkoo rrozadoo*
sweet/dry	doce/seco	*dosee/secoo*
a beer	uma cerveja	*oomah survaheejah*
I'd like to try ... the house wine.	Queria provar ... o vinho da casa.	*kureeah proovar oo veennyo dah kazah*
... mineral water sparkling still	água mineral ... com gás sem gás	*agooah meenural kohm gash saheem gash*
tap water	água da torneira	*agooah dah toornaheerah*

(For more drinks see Café Life, pp75-76.)

on your table

ashtray	o cinzeiro	*oo seenzaheeroo*
bowl	a tigela	*ah teejelah*
cup	a chávena	*ah shavunah*
fork	o garfo	*oo garfoo*
glass	o copo	*oo kopoo*
knife	a faca	*ah fakah*
napkin	o guardanapo	*oo gooahrdahnapoo*
oil	o azeite	*oo ahzaheet*
pepper	a pimenta	*ah peemehntah*
plate	o prato	*oo pratoo*
salt	o sal	*oo sal*
saucer	o pires	*oo peerush*
tablecloth	a toalha de mesa	*ah tooallah du mehzah*
(tea)spoon	a colher (de chá)	*ah kooller (du sha)*
toothpicks	os palitos	*oosh pahleetoosh*
vinegar	o vinagre	*oo veenagru*

check out 3

You ask the waiter for a recommendation.

○ O que me recomenda?
oo ku mu rrukoomehndah

- Recomendamos a caldeirada.
rrukoomehndahmoosh ah kaldaheeradah

○ Pode dizer-me o que é?
pod deezehrmu oo ku e

- Peixe com cebola, tomate e batatas.
paheesh kohm subohlah toomat ee bahtatahsh

Q The dish he recommends includes fish and potatoes:
true or false?

during the meal

you may say …

Excuse me!/Waiter!	(Se) faz favor!/ Por favor!	_(su) fash fah**vohr**/ poor fah**vohr**_
I didn't order …	Não pedi …	_nähoo pu**dee**_
Another (bottle of) …	Mais (uma garrafa de) …	_maheesh (**oo**mah gah**rra**fah du)_
More bread, please.	Mais pão, por favor.	_maheesh pähoo poor fah**vohr**_
Can you bring me …?	Pode trazer-me …?	_pod trah**zehr**mu_
Nothing else, thanks.	Mais nada, obrigado/a.	_maheesh **na**dah obree**ga**doo/ah_
Where are the toilets?	Onde é a casa de banho?	_ohnd e ah **ka**zah du **bahñ**nyoo_
Is smoking allowed?	Pode-se fumar?	_**po**duse foo**mar**_
It's … cold. underdone. delicious!	Está … frio/a. mal passado/a. muito bom/boa!	_eesh**ta** **free**oo/ah mal pah**sa**doo/ah **mooeeñ**too bohm̃/ **boh**ah_
The knife is dirty.	A faca está suja.	_ah **fa**kah eesh**ta** **soo**jah_

Para quem é ... o bife? a salada?	*pah*rah kaheeñ e oo beef ah sah*la*dah	Who is the ... for? steak salad
Está tudo bem?	eesh*ta* **too***doo* baheeñ	Is everything all right?
Como está o/a ...?	*koh*moo eesh*ta* ool ah	How's the ...?
Mais alguma coisa?	maheesh al**goo***mah* **koh***ee*zah	Anything else?

paying

you may say ...

The bill, please.	A conta, se faz favor.	ah **kohn**tah su fash fah**vohr**
Is service included?	Está incluído o serviço?	eesh*ta* eenkloo**ee***doo* oo sur**vee***soo*
Is there a mistake here?	A conta está certa aqui?	ah **kohn**tah eesh*ta* **ser***tah* ah**kee**
We didn't have ... any beer. a dessert.	Não tomámos ... cerveja. sobremesa.	nãhoo too**ma***moosh* sur*va*hee*jah* soobru**meh***zah*
Do you accept credit cards?	Aceita cartões de crédito?	ah**sa***hee*tah kahr**tõ***heesh* du **kre***dee*too

sound check

q is always followed by u. It is said in two different ways.

When qu is followed by a it sounds like 'qua' in 'quack':
quatro *kwa*troo

When qu is followed by e or i it sounds like 'k' in 'keen':
queria ku**ree***ah*   quilo *kee*loo

try it out

question time

Can you select the right answer to these statements?

1 This protects you from spills.

a guardanapo   b garrafa

2 You can eat with these.

a faca e garfo   b sal e pimenta

3 Your food is served in one of these.

a copo   b prato

4 If you can't eat something with nuts, you can say …

a sou alérgico   b sou vegetariano

5 This is the main dish.

a sobremesa   b prato principal

match it up

Match up these twelve halves of words to make six things found in a restaurant (not necessarily to eat or drink).

me	las	ela	lu	mol	so
pa	ho	car	sa	ne	tig

as if you were there

You've just enjoyed a meal in a restaurant in Sintra. Follow the prompts to play your part.

Está tudo bem?

(Say yes, thanks – it's delicious)

(Next, ask for the bill)

Com certeza.

(Ask if they accept credit cards)

Sim, senhor.

(And find out if service is included)

Não, senhor.

(Now say thanks and goodbye)

.....linkup.....

key phrases

O que é caldeirada?	**What is** 'caldeirada'?
Queria salada.	**I would like** salad.
Para mim, o bacalhau.	The cod **for me**.
Traga-me mais pão, se faz favor.	**Could you bring me** more bread, please?
O bife **está** mal passado.	The steak **is** underdone.

ways of saying 'you'

In Portuguese, there are different words for 'you'. The one you use shows your relationship to the person you're speaking to. A waiter may say to you:

E **o senhor**, o que deseja?   And what would you like?
(to a man)
E **a senhora**, o que deseja?   And what would you like?
(to a woman)
as this is a formal/polite situation.

You can also use this to be especially polite. You use você when you've got to know someone a little better, although the word itself is often missed out. Both of these forms have the same verb endings:
O senhor tem filhos?   Do you have children?
(Você) tem filhos?   Do you have children?

And if you are talking to more than one person:
Os senhores têm filhos?/Têm filhos?   Do you (plural) have children?

For more on when to use the different forms of 'you', see the Language Builder, p132. ⋯⋯▷

describing things – ser & estar

Notice the word for 'is' in these two examples:
o garfo **está** sujo the fork **is** dirty
a sopa **está** fria the soup **is** cold

When describing the temporary state of something, use estar
meaning 'to be'. You can also use estar when talking about
things that can change in a relatively short period of time,
such as the weather or the way you feel.
Como **está** o tempo? How **is** the weather?
Estou bem, obrigado. I **am** well, thank you.

If you are talking about essential characteristics and
permanent qualities, use ser:
Sou português. I **am** Portuguese.
O que **é** caldeirada? What **is** 'caldeirada'?

For more on the different verbs for 'to be', see the Language
Builder, pp134-135.

the courses

aperitivos aperitifs
aperitivos e acepipes/entradas/
petiscos starters, snacks
acepipes variados assorted
appetizers
sopas soups
saladas salads
prato principal/segundo prato
main course
peixes fish
mariscos shellfish
carne meat
aves poultry
caça game
legumes vegetables

sobremesas/doces desserts
fruta fruit (for a full list of fruit
and nuts, see p59)
doces desserts

main ways of cooking

à cataplana cooked in a round
copper pan
assado roast
bem passado well done
cozido boiled
cozido ao vapor steamed
escaldado poached
fumado smoked

frito fried
grelhado grilled
mal passado rare, underdone
marinado marinated
no ponto medium done
no churrasco barbecued
no forno in the oven, baked

the menu

açorda thick bread-and-garlic based soup
 de marisco with seafood
 à Alentejana with garlic and herbs
açúcar sugar
aipo celery
alho garlic
amêijoas clams
 à bulhão pato cooked with garlic and coriander
anchovas anchovies
arroz rice
 branco plain
 de ervilhas with peas
 doce rice pudding
 de frango with chicken
 de marisco with seafood
 de manteiga with butter
 e massa and pasta
atum tuna
azeite oil
azeitonas olives
 recheadas stuffed
 pretas black
bacalhau cod
 à Brás with eggs and potatoes
 à Gomes de Sá with black olives, garlic and potatoes
 cozido boiled

batatas ... potatoes
 cozidas boiled
 fritas chips
baunilha vanilla
berinjela aubergine
bife steak (i.e. the cut)
 de atum tuna
 de porco pork
 de vaca beef
bolinhos de amêndoa almond biscuits
bolos cakes
borrego lamb
cabrito kid
cação em vinho tinto fish stew in red wine sauce
caldeirada fish stew
caldo verde soup made with shredded kale, potato and spicy sausage
camarões shrimps
canja de galinha chicken soup
caracóis snails
caranguejo crab
carapau horse-mackerel
carne meat
 de porco à Alentejana pork with clams
carnes frias cold meats
caril curry
castanhas chestnuts
cavala mackerel
cebolas onions
cenouras carrots
cherne turbot
chocolate chocolate
chocos cuttlefish
 com tinta in its ink
chouriço spicy pork sausage, with paprika and garlic

codorniz quail
coelho rabbit
cogumelo mushroom
costeletas chops
couve portuguesa kale
couve-flor cauliflower
cozido à Portuguesa stew
with beef, bacon, sausage
and vegetables
enguia eel
entrecosto rib
ervilhas peas
espadarte swordfish
espargos asparagus
esparguete spaghetti
espetadas kebabs
faisão pheasant
fatias de Braga sweet almond
cake
favas broad beans
feijão verde green beans
feijoada meat and bean stew
fígado com arroz liver with rice
fios Moorish sweetmeat
frango chicken
 na púcura stewed in port,
then fried with wine and
almonds
galinha boiling fowl
gambas king prawns
gaspacho à Alentejana chilled
soup with tomatoes, peppers
cucumbers and onions
gelado ice-cream
grão-de-bico chick peas
hambúrguer burger
iscas (à Portuguesa) liver
(marinated in wine and garlic,
then fried)
javali wild boar

laranja orange
lebre hare
leitão suckling pig
lentilhas lentils
limão lemon
linguado sole
lombo loin (of pork, etc.)
lulas squid
macarrão macaroni
mariscos shellfish
marmelada quince jelly
massa pasta
mel honey
melão melon
 com presunto with ham
mexilhões mussels
migas de bacalhau dried cod
soup with garlic
milho sweetcorn
molho sauce
mousse de chocolate chocolate
mousse
nogado nougat
omeleta omelette
ostras oysters
ovos eggs
 cozidos boiled
 estrelados fried
 mexidos scrambled
pastel de nata/de Belém
custard tart
pastelaria pastries
pato duck
peixe fish
pepino cucumber
perdiz partridge
peru turkey
pescada hake
pêssego peach
picante spicy

pimenta pepper
pimentos peppers
 assados roast
piripiri chilli and olive oil
seasoning
pistacho pistachio
pizza pizza
polvo octopus
porco pork
presunto smoked ham
pudim crème caramel
queijada cheesecake
queijo cheese
rabanetes radishes
repolho white cabbage
rins kidneys
rissóis rissoles
robalo sea-bass
sal salt
salada salad
 de atum tuna
 de feijão black bean
 de tomate tomato
 de alface lettuce
 de frutas fruit
 mista side/mixed
 russa diced vegetables
 and mayonnaise
salmão salmon
santola spider crab
sardinhas sardines
sopa soup
 de hortaliça vegetable soup
 de ervas green vegetable
 soup
 transmontana soup with
 vegetables, bacon and bread
 de peixe fish soup with dry
 bread
tâmaras dates

tamboril monkfish
torta de amêndoa almond tart
tomates tomatoes
tripas tripe
 à moda do Porto Porto style
 (with beans)
truta trout
vagens green beans
veado venison
vinagre vinegar
vitela veal

the drinks

água mineral mineral water
água pé light wine
aguardente brandy
bagaço spirit made from grape
husks
batido milk shake
bica small black coffee (very
strong)
branco/a white (wine)
brandymel honey-brandy
café coffee
 com leite/o garoto small white
 coffee
descafeinado decaffeinated
coffee
caneca draught beer (usually
lager)
cerveja beer/lager
 preta dark beer
chá tea
 com leite/limão tea with
 milk/lemon
 limão herbal lemon tea
chocolate quente hot chocolate
cola cola
 com gás sparkling

com gelo with ice
conhaque cognac
doce sweet
espumante sparkling
fino draught lager (in the north)
fresco/a ice cold
galão white coffee (large, milky, served in a glass)
gin-tónico gin and tonic
Ginjinha spirit distilled from morello cherries
imperial draught lager
laranjada orangeade
leite milk
limonada lemonade
maracujá passion fruit juice
Moscatel sweet dessert wine
natural at room temperature
seco/a dry
sem gás still
sumo juice
 de ananás pineapple
 de fruta fruit
 de laranja orange
 de pêssego peach
 de uva grape
tinto red wine
uísque whisky
vinho wine
 verde 'green' wine (see p71)
 do Porto Port
 da Madeira Madeira

Entertainment

finding out what's on

Local tourist offices can provide details of must-see sights and events. English-language newspapers can also be a good source of information on local and national events. Newsagents' and kiosks in major resorts and the larger towns sell weeklies such as the Algarve-based *Anglo-Portuguese News*. And with even a little knowledge of Portuguese you should be able to make sense of cinema and event listings in the Portuguese press. Try the dailies *Público* and *Diário de Notícias*.

what to see

Football This is the Portuguese national sport, and a live match can be a dramatic and entertaining experience, as can watching a big game in a busy bar. The season runs from September to June, and games are usually on Sundays. One of the biggest teams, Benfica, have the spectacular Estádio da Luz stadium as their homeground (Lisbon, Metro Colégio Militar). Get advance tickets from the kiosk in Praça dos Restauradores.

Bullfights Not everyone's cup of tea, but the Portuguese are proud of the fact that their bullfighters can demonstrate their skills without killing the bulls in the ring. There are bullrings in many southern Portuguese towns; Cascais and Lisbon's Campo Pequeno are two of the biggest. Events tend to be in the evenings and Saturday afternoons from June to September. Tickets can be bought from the venues.

Formula One Portugal's Grand Prix takes place in Estoril, usually in September, and there are practice runs throughout the year.

cinema

Foreign films are nearly always shown in the original-language version with Portuguese subtitles, although the translated titles may be different to the English.

fairs

Portugal is proud of its culture, and most regions go to great lengths to promote traditional song and dance. Look out for performances at local agricultural fairs and festivals, often celebrating saints' days.

music

Tourist offices can provide details of concerts and festivals. Particular to Portugal, don't miss:

Fado Portugal's traditional folk music can be somewhat melancholy but also powerfully moving. Specific fado houses, such as those in Lisbon and Coimbra, have big-name stars, but fado can be at its most appealing when sung spontaneously by a waitress or barman in an intimate café.

Brazilian and African music Clubs in larger Portuguese towns host regular live music nights showcasing these immensely popular musical styles, the legacy of Portugal's colonial days.

sports

Swimming With miles of Atlantic coastline, you're never far from a beach in Portugal. Watch out for strong currents on the west coast; the south-facing Algarve is generally safe.

Most towns have a municipal pool, open from June to September.

Golf Portugal has the perfect climate for golf; there are many courses, most on the Algarve around Vilamoura and Vale do Lobo. Further north there are good courses in Estoril, near Lisbon, and Ponte de Lima.

Tennis There are municipal courts in many towns, which can be booked with 24 hours' notice. You'll also find courts as part of a hotel complex.

Walking The Portuguese are not great walkers, which means that away from a road in rural areas, you're likely to be alone. Walking is excellent in Portugal's National Parks, especially Peneda-Gerês (the Minho), Serra da Estrela (Beira Alta) and Montesinho (Trás-os-Montes). Park offices and local tourist offices can advise on good walking routes and camping spots.

Bird watching Portugal has some unspoilt habitats ideal for migratory birds and waders, especially in its coastal estuaries and mudflats such as at Quinta da Rocha and Rio Formosa in the Algarve, the Tejo nature reserve, and São Jacinto on the Aveiro lagoon in the Beira Litoral.

Picnicking This is a great Portuguese pastime. In summer and at weekends, most parks, beauty spots and **miradouros** (panoramic view points) are busy with sprawling family groups tucking into substantial picnics.

Horseriding Ask at local tourist offices for details. Horse breeding is big business in the Alentejo and the Ribatejo regions, while ponytrekking is popular in Gerês.

Sailing The Portuguese tourist board publishes a brochure detailing Portugal's main sailing facilities and marinas.

Skiing Confined to the mountainous Serra da Estrela, based in Penhas da Saúde.

Fishing and hunting Check in tourist offices or the local **Câmara Municipal** (town hall) regarding permits and equipment hire. Fishing is good both along the coast (resorts such as Lagos in the Algarve offer fishing cruises) and off Madeira, and in Portugal's inland lakes and rivers. Hunting is popular in inland areas where game – even wild boar – is still common.

Surfing A big sport in Portugal; Guincho near Lisbon holds international events, and there are specialised surf centres in Espinho, south of Porto.

children

Portugal is generally a safe and child-friendly country. **Onda parks** (water parks), such as in Caparica outside Lisbon, Beja in the Alentejo and Amarante outside Porto, are popular, as is **Portugal dos Pequenitos**, in Coimbra, a park full of miniature replicas of Portugal's great buildings.

phrasemaker

getting to know the place
you may say ...

Do you have ...	Tem ...	*taheem*
a plan of the town?	uma planta da vila?	*oomah plahntah dah veelah*
an entertainment guide?	um guia de distracções?	*oom geeah du deeshtrasōheesh*
Do you have any information in English?	Tem informações em inglês?	*taheem eenfoormahsōheesh aheem eenglehsh*
What is there to see/do here?	O que se pode ver/fazer aqui?	*oo ku su pod vehr/fahzehr ahkee*
Is there ...	Há ...	*a*
a guided tour?	visita guiada?	*veezeetah geeadah*
a bus tour?	visita de autocarro?	*veezeetah du aootokarroo*
Are there any ... here?	Há ... aqui?	*a ... ahkee*
cinemas	cinemas	*seenehmahsh*
museums	museus	*moozehoosh*
Could you recommend ...	Podia recomendar ...	*poodeeah rrukoomehndar*
a restaurant?	um restaurante?	*oom rrushtaoorahnt*
a club?	uma boîte?	*oomah booat*
an exhibition?	uma exposição?	*oomah aheeshpoozeesāhoo*
a concert?	um concerto?	*oom kohnsehrtoo*
I like ...	Gosto de ...	*goshtoo du*
films.	filmes.	*feelmes*
dancing.	dançar.	*dahnsar*
I prefer ...	Prefiro ...	*prufeeroo*
modern art.	arte moderna.	*art moodernah*
swimming.	nadar.	*nahdar*
Is there anything for children to do?	Há distracções para crianças?	*a deeshtrasōheesh pahrah kreeahãsahsh*

Entertainment

you may hear ...

Há visita guiada.	*a veezeetah geeadah*	There's a guided tour.
Há dois teatros.	*a doheesh teeatroosh*	There are two theatres.
Gosta de ... teatro? andar a cavalo?	*goshtah du teeatroo ahndar ah kavaloo*	Do you like ... theatre? horseriding?
Em que está interessado/a?	*aheem ku eeshta eenturusadoo/ah*	What are you interested in?

things to do or see

art gallery	a galeria de arte	*ah gahlureeah du art*
bullfight	a tourada	*ah tohradah*
cathedral	a catedral	*ah kahtudral*
church	a igreja	*ah eegraheejah*
cinema	o cinema	*oo seenehmah*
fiesta/celebration	a festa	*ah feshtah*
fireworks	os fogos de artifício	*oosh fohgoosh du ahrteefeeseeoo*
funfair	a feira	*ah faheerah*
(football) match	o jogo de (futebol)	*oo johgoo du (footubol)*
park	o parque	*oo park*
stadium	o estádio	*oo eeshtadeeoo*

getting more information

you may say ...

Where is ...	Onde é ...	ohnd e
the swimming pool?	a piscina?	ah peeshseenah
the concert hall?	a sala de concertos?	ah salah du kohnsehrtoosh
the golf course?	o campo de golfe?	oo kampoo du golf
Where are the tennis courts?	Onde são os campos de ténis?	ohnd sãhoo oosh kampoooosh du teneesh
Where does the tour start?	Onde começa a visita?	ohnd koomesah ah veezeetah
What time does it ...	A que horas ...	ah ku orahsh
start?	começa?	koomesah
finish?	termina?	turmeenah
When is it open?	Quando está aberto/a?	kwahñdoo eeshta ahbertoolah
Will I need tickets?	Preciso de bilhetes?	pruseezoo du beellehtush
Are there any tickets?	Há bilhetes?	a beellehtush
Where can I buy tickets?	Onde compro bilhetes?	ohnd kohmproo beellehtush

you may hear ...

Não precisa de bilhetes.	nãhoo pruseezah du beellehtush	You don't need tickets.
Lamento, está esgotado/a.	lahmehntoo eeshta eeshgootadoolah	Sorry, it's sold out.
Na praça principal, às dez horas.	nah prasah preenseepal ash desh orash	In the main square, at 10 o'clock. (See times, p14)
na bilheteira	nah beellutaheerah	at the ticket office
Aqui no mapa.	ahkee noo mapah	Here on the map.

check out 1

You want to go on a day trip to a nearby town.

○ A que horas começa a visita?
ah ku orahsh koomesah ah veezeetah

- Às dez horas.
  ash desh orash

○ A que horas termina?
ah ku orahsh turmeenah

- Às sete da tarde.
  ash set dah tard

 How long does the tour last?

getting in
you may say …

Do you have any tickets?	Tem bilhetes?	*taheem beellehtush*
How much is it?	Quanto é?	***kwañ**too e*
Four tickets, please.	Quatro bilhetes, se faz favor.	***kwa**troo beellehtush su fash fah**vohr***
for …	para …	***pah**rah*
Saturday	sábado	***sa**bahdoo*
tomorrow	amanhã	*amahn**nyãh***
(See days, p17)		
Is there wheelchair access?	Tem acesso para cadeiras de rodas?	*taheem a**se**soo **pah**rah kah**dehee**rahsh du **rro**dash*
Are there any concessions?	Há descontos?	*a deesh**kohn**toosh*

105

May I take photos?	Posso tirar fotografias?	*po*soo tee*rar* footoograh*fee*ahsh
How long does ... last?	Quanto tempo dura ...	*kwañ*too **tehm**poo **doo**rah
the play	a peça (de teatro)?	*ah pesah (du teeatroo)*
the show	o espectáculo?	*oo eeshpetakooloo*
the concert	o concerto?	*oo kohnsehrtoo*
Does the film have subtitles?	O filme tem legendas?	*oo feelm taheñ lujehndahsh*
Is there ...	Há ...	*a*
a programme?	programa?	*proograhmah*
an interval?	intervalo?	*eenturvaloo*
Are the seats numbered?	Estão numerados os lugares?	*eeshtãhoo noomeradoosh ahsh loogaresh*
Is this seat free?	Este lugar está livre?	*ehsht loogar eeshta leevru*

you may hear ...

Sim, para ...	*seeñ pahrah*	Yes, for ...
estudantes.	*eeshtoodahntush*	students.
crianças.	*kreeahnsahsh*	children.
reformados.	*rrufoormadoosh*	seniors.
Demora ...	*dumorah*	It lasts for ...
uma hora.	*oomah orah*	one hour.
três horas.	*trehsh orahsh*	three hours.
um intervalo de vinte minutos	*ooñ eenturvaloo du veent meenootoosh*	one interval of 20 minutes
Está ...	*eeshta*	It's ...
livre.	*leevru*	free.
ocupado.	*okoopadoo*	taken.
plateia	*plahtaheeah*	stalls
balcão	*balkãhoo*	circle
camarote	*kahmahrot*	box
vestiário	*vushteeareeoo*	cloakroom

check out 3

You want to book seats for a show.

○ Tem bilhetes para amanhã?
  taheem beellehtush pahrah amannyāh

- Lamento, está esgotado.
  lahmentoo eeshta eeshgootado

○ Tem bilhetes para sábado?
  taheem beellehtush pahrah sabahdoo

- Sim, senhor.
  seem sunnyohr

 What day can you see the show?

swimming & sunbathing

you may say ...

Where can I go swimming?	Onde posso ir nadar?	*ohnd **po**soo eer nah**dar***
Is it safe for children?	É seguro para crianças?	*e see**goo**roo **pah**rah kree**ãhn**sash*
Can I use the hotel pool?	Posso usar a piscina do hotel?	***po**soo oo**zar** ah peesh**see**nah doo o**tel***
Where are the ... changing rooms? showers?	Onde são os ... vestiários? chuveiros?	*ond **sãhoo** oosh vushteea**ree**oosh shoo**vahee**roosh*
I'd like a towel.	Queria uma toalha.	*ku**ree**ah **oo**mah too**allah***
I'd like to hire ... a sunlounger.	Queria alugar ... uma espreguiçadeira.	*ku**ree**ah ahloo**gar** **oo**mah eeshprugee-sah**dahee**rah*
a parasol. a deck chair.	um guardasol. uma cadeira de lona.	*oom gooardah**sol** **oo**mah kah**dahee**rah du **loh**nah*

sports
you may say ...

Where can I play ...	Onde posso jogar ...	*ohnd* **po***soo joo***gar**
tennis?	ténis?	**te***neesh*
golf?	golfe?	*golf*
volleyball?	voleibol?	*volahee***bol**
Where can I go ...	Onde posso ir fazer ...	*ohnd* **po***soo eer* **fah***zer*
climbing?	alpinismo?	*alpee***neesh***moo*
riding?	equitação?	*ehkeetah***sã***hoo*
walking?	excursões a pé?	*eeshkoo***sõheesh** *ah pe*
I'd like to hire ...	Queria alugar ...	*ku***ree***ah ahloo***gar**
a racket.	uma raqueta.	**oo***mah rrah***ke***tah*
waterskis.	esquis aquáticos.	*eesh***keesh** *ah***koo***a***tee***koosh*
rollerblades.	patins em linha.	*pah***teensh** *ahee***m** **leen***nyah*
I'd like to take ... lessons.	Queria ter lições de ...	*ku***ree***ah tehr lee***sõheesh** *du*
sailing	vela.	**ve***lah*
windsurfing	wind-surf.	*weend***surf**
surfing	surf.	*surf*
waterskiing	esqui aquático.	*eesh***kee** *ah***koo***a***tee***koo*
How much is it per day/hour?	Quanto é por dia/hora?	**kwañ***too e poor* **dee***a/o***ra**
snowboarding	fazer snowboard	*fah***zer** *snowboard*
skiing	esquiar	*eehsh***kee***ar*
scuba diving	mergulhar	*meergool***lar**

you may hear ...

| São vinte euros por hora. | *sãhoo veentee eoorosh poor ora* | It's €20 per hour. |

sports equipment

boots	as botas	*ahsh botahsh*
dinghy/sailing boat	o barco à vela	*oo barkoo a velah*
golf clubs	os tacos de golfe	*oosh takoosh du golf*
surfboard	a prancha de surf	*ah prahnshah du surf*
tennis balls	as bolas de ténis	*ahsh bolahsh du teneesh*
tennis racket	a raqueta de ténis	*ah rahketah du teneesh*
windsurf board	a prancha à vela/ de wind-surf	*ah prahnshah a velah/du weendsurf*

sound check

When **o** is stressed, or when it has an acute accent, it sounds like 'o' in 'pot':

jogo *johgoo*   golfe *golf*

óculos *okooloosh*

When it's not stressed, it sounds like 'oo' in 'cook':

barco *barkoo*

õ with an accent is a nasal sound.

excursões *eeshkoosõheesh*

try it out

lost for words

E	S	P	E	C	T	A	C	U	L	O
S	B	H	X	N	A	L	Z	E	V	I
Q	O	C	P	G	M	E	D	S	B	R
U	L	M	O	E	J	V	A	U	C	A
I	F	E	S	T	A	I	H	M	G	I
S	R	A	I	O	D	S	L	F	O	T
D	U	K	C	A	Y	I	A	N	L	S
E	S	C	A	D	A	T	O	H	F	E
P	Q	U	O	I	D	A	T	S	E	V

There are thirteen words hidden in the grid. They are all places to visit, activities or sports and leisure equipment. Words go up and down, backwards and forwards, and diagonally. The first two have been done for you.

match it up
Can you match up the following words on the left and right to make sports equipment or things you might use on the beach?

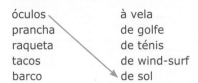

óculos	à vela
prancha	de golfe
raqueta	de ténis
tacos	de wind-surf
barco	de sol

110

in the mix

Use the clues to help you unscramble these words:

1 this activity will get you to the top: **alpimonis**
2 picture palace: **macine**
3 essential furniture for holiday activity! **preguiçaesdeira**
4 place where works of art are displayed: **legaria**
5 none left: **gotadoes**
6 now you can follow the film: **genledas**
7 time to stretch your legs and visit the bar! **interlova**
8 downstairs seating in a theatre: **teiapla**

as if you were there

You're staying near a large hotel, and ask about the pool.
Follow the prompts to play your part.

(Ask if you can use the hotel pool)
Sim, senhor. São quatro euros por dia.
(Say you'd like to hire a sunlounger)
São sete euros no total. Tem toalha?
(Say yes and thank her. Next ask where the showers are)
Ao lado da saída.

linkup

Há uma piscina?	**Is there** a swimming pool?
Não gosto de museus.	**I don't like** museums.
Onde se pode pescar?	**Where can you** fish?
Preciso de bilhetes?	**Do I need** tickets?
A que horas abre?	**What time does it open**?

likes, dislikes & preferences

To say you like something, use gosto de:
Gosto de música salsa. I like salsa music.
Gosto de desporto. I like sport.

To say you don't like something, add não:
Não gosto de nadar. I don't like swimming.

And you can express stronger feelings:
Gosto muito de andar de bicicleta. I really like cycling.
Adoro futebol. I love football.

can & can't

If you want to find out what you can and can't do in a place,
the easiest way is to use the verb poder:
Posso pescar aqui? Can I fish here?
Onde **podemos** nadar? Where can we swim?

To ask what you can do in a more general sense, use se
pode/pode-se:
O que **se pode** ver aqui? What is there to see here?
Onde é que **se pode** jogar golfe? Where can you play golf?
Pode-se fumar aqui? Can you smoke here?

Emergencies

reporting crime

Violent crime is rare in Portugal, but it pays to take sensible precautions wherever you stay, and not to leave valuables unattended. If you have something stolen, report the incident to the nearest **esquadra** (police station) as soon as possible. For emergencies phone 112. The police can issue a written report for insurance claims.

health

You don't need to take any precautions against specific illnesses in Portugal, and drinking water is perfectly safe. Should you become ill, most towns have a **farmácia** (chemist's); opening hours are the same as shops. They can advise on general ailments and point you to the nearest doctor if one is necessary; be prepared to wait some time to see one and to pay for treatment (although this can be claimed back on insurance).

In an emergency, dial 112 and you will be taken to the nearest hospital, but be warned that these vary in quality. EU nationals with an EHIC card are entitled to free emergency treatment. Apply for one at **www.ehic.org.uk** or pick up a form in UK post offices.

car breakdown

You'll find emergency telephones every mile or so on motorways. If taking your own car, find out if your automobile recovery service has a reciprocal agreement with the **Automóvel Clube de Portugal**. Otherwise check with your hirer.

making calls

Public phone boxes can be found in most Portuguese towns and villages, and take coins or a **cartão credifone** (phone card). Phone cards are available in €5 or €10 from post offices or newsagent's. Public phones can also be found in bars and cafés.

post offices

Correios (post offices) can be found in nearly any Portuguese town, and they accept **posta restante** mail (sometimes for a small fee). For stamps, look for the counter marked **selos**. (See buying stamps, p66.)

travellers with disabilities

Disabled facilities are improving in Portugal, although far from ideal. The Portuguese Tourist Board or local tourist office can provide a list of hotels that have wheelchair access. The Orange Badge symbol is recognised for disabled car parking. Lisbon airport also offers a service for wheelchair users, although advance notice is required.

useful contacts

Emergencies 112 (**SOS** – Serviço Nacional de Emergências)

Directory enquiries 118 (automated service); 12118 (to speak to an operator)

Yellow Pages (Páginas Amarelas) **www.pai.pt**.

Tourist Information 808 781 212

Airport information
(+351) 218 413 500 (Lisbon)
(+351) 229 432 400 (Porto)
(+351) 289 800 800 (Faro)
www.ana-aeroportos.pt.

phrasemaker

general phrases
you may say …

Help!	Socorro!	*sohkohrroo*
Excuse me!/Hello there!	Desculpe!	*dushkoolp*
Can you help me?	Pode ajudar-me?	*pod ahjoodarmu*
It's urgent.	É urgente.	*e oorjehnt*
Where is …	Onde é …	*ohnd e*
the police station?	a esquadra?	*ah eeshkwadrah*
the hospital?	o hospital?	*oo oshpeetal*
Where is (the nearest) …	Onde é … (mais próxima)?	*ohnd e … (maeesh proseemah)*
petrol station?	a estação de serviço	*ah eeshtahsãhoo du surveesoo*
garage?	a garagem	*ah gahrajaheem̃*
phone?	a telefone	*ah tehlehfon*
chemist's?	a farmácia	*ah fahrmaseeah*
Is there someone here who speaks English?	Há alguém aqui que fale inglês?	*a algaheem̃ ahkee ku fal eenglehsh*
thank you	obrigado/a	*obreegadoo/ah*
Leave me alone!	Deixe-me em paz!	*daheeshumu aheem̃ pash*
I'll call the police.	Chamo a polícia.	*shahmoo ah pooleeseeah*

health
you may say …

I'd like an appointment with …	Queria uma consulta com …	*kureeah oomah kohnsooltah kohm̃*
a doctor.	um medico.	*oom̃ medeekoo*
a dentist.	um dentista.	*oom̃ dehnteeshtah*
I need …	Preciso …	*pruseezoo*
a doctor.	dum médico.	*doom̃ medeekoo*
an ambulance.	duma ambulância.	*doomah ahmboolahnseeah*

My ... hurts.	Dói-me o/Tenho dor de ...	*doeemu oo/taheennyoo dohr du*
stomach	estômago.	*eeshtohmahgoo*
My eyes hurt.	Doem-me os olhos.	*doehmmu oosh olloosh*
It hurts here.	Dói aqui.	*doee ahkee*
I have ...	Tenho dor de ...	*taheennyoo dohr du*
toothache.	dentes.	*dehntush*
a sore throat.	garganta.	*gahrgahntah*
a headache.	cabeça.	*kahbehsah*
Is it serious?	É grave?	*e grav*
I can't ... my leg.	Não posso ... a perna.	*nãhoo posoo ... ah purnah*
move	mexer	*mushehr*
feel	sentir	*sehnteer*
I've been sick.	Vomitei.	*voomeetahee*
My son/My daughter has a temperature.	O meu filho/A minha filha tem febre.	*oo mehoo feelloo/ah meennyah feellah taheem febr*
She/He feels sick.	Tem náuseas.	*taheem naoozeeahsh*
I've got ...	Tenho ...	*taheennyoo*
a cold (virus).	constipação.	*kohnshteepahsãhoo*
constipation.	prisão de ventre.	*preezãhoo du vehntru*
a cough.	tosse.	*tos*
I've cut/burnt myself.	Cortei-me/Queimei-me.	*koortaheemu/kaheemaheemu*
I've been bitten by a dog.	Fui mordido/a por um cão.	*fooee moordeedoo/ah poor oom kãhoo*

I've been bitten by an insect.	Fui picado/a por um insecto.	*fooee peekadoo/ah poor oom eensetoo*
I've lost a filling.	Perdi um chumbo.	*purdee oom shoomboo*
I'm allergic to ... antibiotics. animals.	Sou alérgico/a a ... antibióticos. animais.	*soh ahlerjeekoo/ah ah ahnteebeeoteekoosh ahneemaeesh*
I'm ... diabetic. epileptic. HIV positive.	Sou ... diabético/a. epiléptico/a. HIV positivo.	*soh deeahbeteekoo/ah ehpeeleteeko/ah aga ee veh poozeeteevoo*
I'm pregnant.	Estou grávida.	*eeshtoh graveedah*
I have asthma.	Sofro de asma.	*sohfroo du ashmah*
I wear contact lenses.	Uso lentes de contacto.	*oozoo lehntush du kohntatoo*

you may hear ...

Qual é o problema?	*kwal e oo problehmah*	What is the problem?
Há quanto tempo se sente assim?	*a kwahñtoo tehmpoo su sehnt ahseem*	How long have you been feeling like this?
Vou examiná-lo/-la.	*voh eezahmeenaloo/lah*	I'm going to examine you.
Dispa-se, se faz favor.	*deeshpahsu su fash fahvohr*	Please undress.
Deite-se ali.	*daheetusu ahlee*	Lie down there.
Onde lhe dói?	*ond llu doee*	Where does it hurt?
Não é grave.	*nãhoo e grav*	It's not serious.
O osso está partido.	*oo ohsoo eeshta pahrteedoo*	The bone is broken.
É preciso fazer uma operação.	*e pruseezoo fahzehr oomah oprahsãhoo*	You will need an operation.
Isto é uma receita.	*eeshtoo e oomah rrusaheetah*	This is a prescription.
Vou meter-lhe um chumbo (provisório).	*voh mutehrllu oom shoomboo (prooveezorreeo)*	I'll put in a (temporary) filling.
Tenho de tirar-lhe este dente.	*taheennyoo du teerarllu ehsht dehnt*	I'll have to take this tooth out.

check out 1

You go to see a doctor about your stomach pain.

○ Dói-me o estômago.
doeemu oo eeshtohmahgoo

- Deite-se ali – vou examiná-lo ... Não é grave.
Isto é uma receita.
daheetusu ahlee. voh ehzahmeenaloo. nãhoo e grav.
eeshtoo e oomah rrusaheetah

 The doctor says you need to go to hospital: true or false?

at the chemist's

you may say ...

Do you have something for ...	Tem alguma coisa para ...	*taheem algoomah koheezah pahrah*
travel sickness?	enjoo?	*ehnjohoo*
diarrhoea?	diarreia?	*deeahrraheeah*
sunstroke?	insolação?	*eensoolahsãhoo*
sunburn?	queimadura solar?	*keheemadurah solahr*
Do you have any ...	Tem ...	*taheem*
after-sun lotion?	loção pós-sol?	*loosãhoo posh-sol*
anti-histamine?	anti-histamina?	*ahntee-eeshtahmeenah*
aspirin?	aspirinas?	*ahshpeereenahsh*
baby food?	comida para bebé?	*koomeedah pahrah bebe*
condoms?	preservativos?	*pruhzurvahteevoosh*
insect repellent?	repelente para insectos?	*rupulehnt pahrah eensetoosh*
plasters?	adesivos?	*ahduzeevoosh*
paracetamol?	paracetamol?	*pahrahseetahmol*
sun cream?	creme para bronzear?	*krem pahrah brohnzeear*

you may hear ...

Portuguese	Pronunciation	English
O que comeu/bebeu?	oh ku koomeoo/bubeoo	What have you eaten/drunk?
Está a tomar outro medicamento?	eshtah ah toomar ahlgooma mehdeekamehntoo	Are you taking any other medication?
Tome ...	tom	Take ...
estes comprimidos.	ehshtush kohmpreemeedoosh	these pills/tablets.
este xarope para a tosse.	ehsht shahrop pahrah ah tos	this cough mixture.
este medicamento.	ehsht mehdeekamehntoo	this medicine.
Aplique ...	ahpleek	Apply ...
esta loção.	eshtah loosãhoo	this lotion.
este creme.	ehsht krem	this cream.
... por dia	poor deeah	... a day
uma vez	oomah vehsh	once
duas vezes	dooahsh vehzush	twice
três vezes	trehsh vehzush	three times
... refeições	rrufaheesõheesh	... meals
antes das	ahntush dahsh	before
depois das	dupoheesh dahsh	after
com água	kohm agooah	with water
Mastigue, não engula inteiro.	mahshteegu nãhoo ehngoolah ehntaheeroo	Chew, don't swallow whole.
não morda	nãhoo mohrdah	don't bite
Deve ...	dev	You must ...
descansar.	dushkahnsar	rest.
dormir.	doormeer	sleep.
Não deve ...	nãhoo dev	You mustn't ...
levantar-se.	luvahntarsu	get up.
correr.	koorrehr	run.
fazer exercício.	fahzehr ehzurseeseeoo	take exercise.

parts of the body

ankle	o tornozelo	*oo toornoozehloo*
arm	o braço	*oo brasoo*
back	as costas	*ahsh koshtahsh*
chest	o peito	*oo paheetoo*
ear (outer/inner)	a orelha/o ouvido	*ah orehllah/ oo ohveedoo*
eye(s)	o olho/os olhos	*oo ohlloo/oosh olloosh*
foot	o pé	*oo pe*
hand	a mão	*ah mãhoo*
hip	a anca	*ah ahnkah*
knee	o joelho	*oo jooehlloo*
leg	a perna	*ah pernah*
neck	o pescoço	*oo pushkohsoo*
shoulder	o ombro	*oo ohmbroo*
thigh	a coxa	*ah kohshah*

check out 2

You need to sort out a worrying holiday illness.

○ Tem alguma coisa para diarreia?
taheem algoomah koheezah pahrah deeahrraheeah

- Sim, senhora. Tome estes comprimidos, com água, três vezes por dia.
seem sunnyohrah. tom ehshtush kohmpreemeedoosh kohm agooah trehsh vehzush poor deeah

○ Antes das refeições?
ahntush dahsh rrufaheesõheesh

- Não. Depois das refeições.
nãhoo dupoheesh dahsh rrufaheesõheesh

○ Obrigada.
obreegadah

 How should you take the pills?

120

toiletries

deodorant	o desodorizante	*oo duzodooreezahnt*
contact lens solution	o líquido para lentes de contacto	*oo leekeedoo pahrah lehntush du kohntatoo*
nappies	as fraldas	*ahsh fraldahsh*
razor blades	as lâminas de barbear	*ash lahmeenahsh du bahrbeear*
shampoo	o champô	*o shampoh*
sanitary towels	os pensos higiénicos	*oosh pehñsoosh eejeeeeneekoosh*
tampons	os tampões	*oosh tahmpõheesh*
toothbrush	a escova de dentes	*ah eeshkohvah du dehntush*
toothpaste	a pasta de dentes	*ah pashtah du dehntush*

car breakdown

you may say …

I've broken down on the motorway E4.	Tive uma avaria na auto-estrada E4.	*teev oomah ahvahreeah nah aootoeeshtradah eh kwatroo*
five kilometres from …	a cinco quilómetros de …	*ah seeñkoo keelomutroosh du*
… isn't working. The engine The steering	… não funciona. O motor A direcção	*nãhoo foonseeohnah oo mootohr ah deeresãhoo*
The brakes aren't working.	Os travões não funcionam.	*oosh trahvõheesh nãhoo foonseeohnahm̃*
I have a flat tyre.	Tenho um pneu furado.	*taheennyoo oom̃ punehoo fooradoo*
I've run out of petrol.	Acabou-se-me a gasolina.	*ahkahbohsumu ah gahzooleenah*
When will it be ready?	Quando estará pronto?	*kwahñdo eeshtahra prohntoo*

you may hear ...

Qual é o problema?	*kwal e oo problehmah*	What's the problem?
Onde está, exactamente?	*ohnd eeshta ehzatahmehnt*	Where are you exactly?
Demoramos uma hora.	*dumoorahmoosh oomah orah*	We'll be with you in an hour. (See times, p14)
Está pronto na próxima sexta.	*eeshta prohntoo nah proseemah sehshtah*	It'll be ready next Friday. (See days, p17)

check out 3

You've had a breakdown, and phone a garage for help.

○ Tive uma avaria.
teev oomah ahvahreeah

- Qual é o problema?
kwal e oo prooblehmah

○ A embriagem não funciona.
ah ehmbraeeajaheem nãhoo foonseeohnah

- Demoramos uma hora.
dumoorahmoosh oomah orah

Q You have a flat tyre: true or false?

car parts

accelerator	o acelerador	*oo ahsulahrah**dohr***
battery	a bateria	*ah bahtu**ree**ah*
brakes	os travões	*oosh trah**voh**eesh*
clutch	a embriagem	*ah ehmbrae**ea**jaheem̃*
radiator	o radiador	*oo rradeeah**dohr***
steering wheel	o volante	*oo voo**lahn**t*
tyres	os pneus	*oosh pune**hoosh***
wheels	as rodas	*ahsh **rro**dahsh*
windows	as janelas	*ahsh jah**ne**lahsh*
windscreen wiper	o limpador de pára-brisas	*oo leempah**dohr** du **pa**rah-**bree**zahsh*

theft or loss
you may say …

I've lost …	Perdi …	*pur**dee***
my wallet.	a minha carteira.	*ah **meen**nyah kahr**ta**heerah*
my passport.	o meu passaporte.	*oo **me**hoo pasah**port***
I've had my … stolen.	Roubaram-me o meu …	*rroh**ba**rahm̃ mu oo **me**hoo*
watch	relógio.	*rru**lo**jeeoo*
bag	saco.	***sa**koo*
I've been …	Fui …	*fooee*
mugged.	roubado/a.	*rroh**ba**doo/ah*
attacked.	atacado/a.	*ahta**ka**do/ah*
Our car has been broken into.	O nosso carro foi assaltado.	*oo **no**soo **ka**rroo fohee ahsal**ta**doo*
last night/ this morning	ontem à noite/ hoje de manhã	***ohn**taheem̃ a noheet/ ohj du man**nyah̃***
in the street/in a shop	na rua/numa loja	*nah **rroo**ah/**noo**mah **lo**jah*
It's …	É …	*e*
large.	grande.	*grand*
blue.	azul.	*a**zool***
made of leather.	de couro.	*du **koh**ooroo*

you may hear ...

Que aconteceu?	*ku ahkohntusehoo*	What happened?
Quando ...?	**kwahñ**doo	When ...?
Onde ...?	*ohnd*	Where ...?
Como é?	**koh**moo e	What does it look like?
Qual é ...	*kwal e*	What is ...
o seu nome?	*oo **seh**oo nohm*	your name?
a sua morada?	*a **soo**ah moor**a**dah*	your address?
a sua matrícula?	*ah **soo**ah mah**tree**koolah*	your car registration?
o número do seu passaporte?	*oo **noo**muroo doo **seh**oo pasah**port***	your passport number?
Preencha este impresso.	*pree**ehn**shah ehsht eem**pre**soo*	Fill in this form.
Volte mais tarde.	*volt maheesh tard*	Come back later.

valuables

briefcase	a pasta	*ah **pash**tah*
(digital) camera	a câmara (digital)	*ah **kah**mahrah (deejee**tal**)*
credit cards	os cartões de crédito	*oosh kahr**tõheesh** du **kre**deetoo*
driving licence	a carta de condução	*ah **kar**tah du kohndoo**sãhoo***
handbag	o saco de mão	*oo **sa**koo du mãhoo*
jewellery	as jóias	*ahsh **joee**ahsh*
money	o dinheiro	*oo deen**nyahee**roo*
purse/wallet	a carteira	*ah kahr**tahee**rah*
suitcase	a mala	*ah **ma**lah*
laptop	o computador portátil	*oo kohmpootah**dohr** poor**ta**teel*
mobile phone	o telemóvel	*oo tele**mo**vel*
mp3 player	o leitor de mp3	*oo lahee**tohr** du em peh trehsh*

check out 4
You report a robbery at the police station.

○ Roubaram-me o meu saco.
rrohbarahṁmu oo mehoo sakoo

- Quando?
kwahñdoo

○ Hoje de manhã.
ohj du mannyãh

- Onde?
ohnd

○ Na rua Barata.
nah rrooah bahratah

- Preencha este impresso, se faz favor.
prreeehnshah ehsht eempresoo su fash fahvohr

Q When was your bag stolen?
What are you asked to do?

sound check

s at the beginning of a word or after a consonant, is pronounced like 's' in 'sit':
se faz favor *su fash fahvohr*

s at the end of a word or before **c**, **f**, **p**, **q** or **t**, is pronounced like 'sh' in 'she':
mais *maeesh*

ç, or **c** followed by **e** or **i** sound like 's' in 'sit':
polícia *pooleeseeah*   emergências *eemurjehnseeahsh*

c followed by anything else sounds like 'k' in 'kit':
começa *koomesah*   cara *karah*

question time

The following questions have the spaces between the words in the wrong places. See if you can rearrange them and understand what they mean.

1 Háal gué maqui quefa leing lês?
2 On del hed ói?
3 Temas piri nas?
4 Quan does taráp ron to?
5 Qua léo se uno me?

match it up

Match up the halves of the sentences below to make complete sentences. They're all things you might say to a doctor or in an emergency.

Chamo	o meu relógio.
Preciso	tosse.
Queria	o dedo.
Tenho	a polícia.
Não posso mexer	uma consulta.
Perdi	duma ambulância.

as if you were there

On holiday in the Algarve, you need to visit the dentist. Follow the prompts to play your part.

Qual é o problema?
(Tell the dentist you've lost a filling and have a toothache)
Vou examiná-lo. Deite-se ali ...
(Ask if it's serious)
Não. Vou meter-lhe um chumbo provisório.
(Say thank you)

linkup

Pode ajudar-me?	**Can you** help me?
Preciso dum médico.	**I need** a doctor.
Tenho dor de garganta.	**I have** a sore throat.
Dói-me o estômago.	**My** stomach hurts.
Tem alguma coisa para a tosse?	**Do you have anything for** a cough?
Tenho um pneu furado.	**I have** a flat tyre.
Estou na estrada para Coimbra.	**I'm** on the road to Coimbra.
Perdi o meu passaporte.	**I've lost** my passport.

saying what hurts

There are two simple ways of expressing pain. You can use dói-me:

Dói-me a cabeça. My head **hurts**. (literally, It hurts me the head)

This changes to doem-me when talking about more than one thing:

Doem-me os pés. My legs **hurt**. (literally, They hurt me the feet)

Or you can say:

Tenho dor de cabeça. **I have a** head**ache**. (literally, I have pain of the head)

The word de is also very useful when linking two words to describe something:

uma camisa de algodão a cotton shirt (literally, a shirt of cotton)
óculos de sol sunglasses (literally, glasses of sun)

saying what's yours

To say something belongs to you say:

o meu bilhete **my** ticket (for masculine singular words)
a minha morada **my** address (for feminine singular words)
os meus filhos **my** sons/children (for masculine plural words)
as minhas chaves **my** keys (for feminine plural words)

For how to say 'your', 'his', 'their' and 'our', see the Language Builder, p131. For how to say 'your', 'his', 'their' and 'our', see the Language Builder, p131.

Language **Builder**

The words and phrases in this book will enable you to get by in Portuguese in everyday situations, but to communicate further you'll need to start creating your own sentences. This section shows you how.

articles: 'a' & 'the'

There are two words for 'a' in Portuguese, um and uma. You say um café but uma cerveja. This is because the words for all Portuguese things or people (nouns) are either masculine or feminine.

Um goes with masculine words and uma with feminine words. It is not always easy to know whether a noun is masculine or feminine, but in general nouns ending in **-o** are masculine, and those ending in **-a** are feminine:

um castelo a castle   uma loja a shop
um apartamento a flat   uma camisa a shirt

The plural of 'a' (some) is expressed by uns (m) or umas (f), as well as by the words alguns (m) and algumas (f):

uns castelos some castles
alguns apartamentos some flats
umas lojas some shops
algumas camisas some shirts

There are four words for 'the'. Again, the right one depends on whether the word it refers to is masculine or feminine, singular or plural:

o cinto (m) the belt   **a** sardinha (f) the sardine
os cintos (mpl) the belts   **as** sardinhas (fpl) the sardines

singular & plural

When you are talking about more than one person or thing, you normally add an **s** to the word:

rapariga, raparigas girl, girls
azeitona, azeitonas olive, olives

cebola, cebolas onion, onions
sapato, sapatos shoe, shoes

There are some exceptions to this rule, which are important because they often apply to common words:

words ending in -r or -z

ascensor, ascensores lift, lifts
senhor, senhores man, men
cartaz, cartazes poster, posters

words ending in -m

jardim, jardins garden, gardens
pudim, pudins pudding, puddings

words ending in -ão

galão, galões white coffee, coffees
ladrão, ladrões thief, thieves
mão, mãos hand, hands
pão, pães bread roll, rolls

words ending in -al, -el, -ol, -il

postal, postais stamp, stamps
hotel, hotéis hotel, hotels
lençol, lençóis sheet, sheets
réptil, répteis reptile, reptiles

adjectives

These describing words have different endings, depending on whether the noun they describe is masculine or feminine, singular or plural. Here, the adjective is the word for 'dirty': sujo. Notice how it changes:

um carro suj**o** a dirty car
uma faca suj**a** a dirty knife

In most cases the **o** at the end of the adjective changes to an **a** to make it feminine.

If the noun is plural, the ending of the adjective must agree:
os pimentos vermelh**os** red peppers
as maçãs vermelh**as** red apples

In general, unlike in English, the adjective is placed after the noun.

Words for talking about possession e.g. 'my' and 'your', are adjectives, and so change according to the noun they describe:

	masc.	fem.	m. plural	f. plural
my	**o meu** carro	**a minha** casa	**os meus** sapatos	**as minhas** gambas
your	**o seu** carro	**a sua** casa	**os seus** sapatos	**as suas** gambas
our	**o nosso** carro	**a nossa** casa	**os nossos** sapatos	**as nossas** gambas

Another way to say something belongs to someone is to use do (which changes to da in front of singular feminine nouns, and dos or das in front of masculine or feminine plural nouns):
o carro do meu amigo my friend's car
(literally, the car of my friend)
a casa dos meus pais my parents' house
(literally, the house of my parents)

this, that, these, those

Once again, the right word always depends on whether the object you are pointing out is masculine or feminine, singular or plural. This is because you are using a type of adjective.

this, these (near to the person speaking)
este melão, estes melões this melon, these melons
esta saia, estas saias this skirt, these skirts

that, those (near the person you are talking to)
esse melão, esses melões that melon, those melons
essa saia, essas saias that skirt, those skirts

that, those over there (away from both parties)
aquele melão, aqueles melões that melon, those melons
aquela saia, aquelas saias that skirt, those skirts

pointing out
If you don't know the name of something you want to buy,
you can always point and say:
um destes one of these
um desses one of those (near the person you are talking to)
um daqueles one of those (over there)

talking to people

There are a few words for 'you' in Portuguese. It depends
on who you are talking to. For example, if you are talking
to a stranger it is best to be polite and say o senhor (to a
man) or a senhora (to a woman). You do the same in formal
situations, even if you already know the person.

Once you have become friendly with someone you can
use the more informal você (to men or women). There
is a third word, tu, which you should only use for very
close friendships. Families and close friends use it among
themselves, or if talking to children. You will also hear people
using o and a and a first name, e.g. o Miguel, a Ana.

verbs

Verbs, which are the words that express actions, change
their endings frequently, far more than in English. What
makes them change their endings is the person who is doing
the action. Look at the example for the verb falar (to speak),
on the next page. These endings are for regular verbs ending
in -ar.

falar: to speak	
fal**o**	I speak
fal**as**	you speak (very informal only, 'tu' form)
fal**a**	you speak; he/she/it speaks
fal**amos**	we speak
fal**am**	you (plural) speak; they speak

There are two other common patterns of verbs: those ending in -er and those ending in -ir. The following examples show the endings of regular verbs of these types.

comer: to eat	
com**o**	I eat
com**es**	you eat (very informal, 'tu' form)
com**e**	you eat; he/she/it eats
com**emos**	we eat
com**em**	you (plural) eat; they eat

abrir: to open	
abr**o**	I open
abr**es**	you open (very informal, 'tu' form)
abr**e**	you open; he/she/it opens
abr**imos**	we open
abr**em**	you (plural) open; they open

Verbs that follow the patterns above are called regular verbs. However, many of the common verbs are irregular verbs and must be learnt individually.

Some regular verbs: morar (to live), trabalhar (to work), pagar (to pay), comprar (to pay), experimentar (to try on), levar (to take), beber (to drink), partir (to leave), ficar (to be found/located) .

Some irregular verbs: ser, estar, (to be), ter (to have), ir (to go), dizer (to say), trazer (to bring) and poder (to be able to).

ter: to have	
tenho	I have
tens	you have (very informal only, 'tu' form)
tem	you have; he/she/it has
temos	we have
têm	you (plural) have; they have

ir: to go	
vou	I go
vais	you go (very informal only, 'tu' form)
vai	you go; he/she/it goes
vamos	we go
vão	you (plural) go; they go

poder: to be able to	
posso	I can/may
podes	you can/may (very informal, 'tu' form)
pode	you can/may; he/she/it can/may
podemos	we can/may
podem	you (plural) can/may; they can/may

the verb 'to be'

There are three quite different verbs that express 'am', 'is' and 'are': they are: ser, estar and ficar. (There is a fourth way of saying 'is' or 'are' – há – which means 'there is' or 'there are'.)

A água está fria! The water is cold!

Onde estão os meus sapatos? Where are my shoes?

In these two examples you use estar because you are talking about states that can change (you were perhaps hoping the water was warm; and the shoes are not where you expected).

São americanos. They are American.

Onde é a igreja? Where is the church?

Here you use ser because you are talking about a permanent quality (the fact that they are American), and a fixed location.

Onde fica a igreja? Where is the church?
Fica longe? Is it far?

When talking about location you can also use ficar (to be found/located).

pronouns

You may have noticed that the words for 'I', 'you', 'he', 'she', 'we' and 'they' are not generally used in Portuguese. They do exist, but the only time you will really need them is when you need to say the right word for 'you': o senhor, a senhora, você and tu, or for emphasis (*I'm* not going).

If you are having difficulty in making yourself understood, you may wish to use the pronouns to make it clear.
Here is the full list:

I	eu
you (very informal)	tu
you (quite friendly)	você
you (polite)	o senhor/a senhora
he/it	ele
she/it	ela
we	nós
you (plural, quite friendly)	vocês
you (plural, polite)	os senhores/as senhoras
they	eles/elas

Here are some examples:
Eu chamo-me Paulo, e você? My name is Paulo, and you?
Elas são inglesas. They (**feminine**) are English.

negatives

To make a statement negative, simply put the word não before
the verb:

Não sou francesa. I'm not French.
Não moro em Lisboa. I don't live in Lisbon.
Não gosto de peixe. I don't like fish.
Não compreendo. I don't understand.

questions

Asking questions is not difficult – you can simply state what
you want in a questioning way. For example:

Tem quartos vagos. You have free rooms.
Tem quartos vagos? Do you have any free rooms? (said with
rising intonation towards the end of the sentence)

You may often want to ask specific questions with words like
'when', 'where' and 'how'. Here is a list of question words:

Onde ...? Where ...?
Quando ...? When ...?
Como ...? How ...?
Quem ...? Who ...?
Porque ...? Why ...?
Que ...? What ...?
Quanto ...? How much ...?
Qual ...? Which ...?
A que horas? What time?

Answers

Bare Necessities.......

check out
1 tomorrow
2 afternoon; false, you're on business
3 £200

lucky numbers

5 = cinco
15 = quinze
125 = cento e vinte e cinco
39 = trinta e nove
51 = cinquenta e um
311 = trezentos e onze
1000 = mil

lost in translation

1 Trabalho em Londres.
2 Falo inglês e português.
3 Desculpe!
4 Onde é o elevador?
5 Queria um café.
6 Quanto custa o livro?
7 Não compreendo.

as if you were there

Chamo-me Anna.
*shah*moomu anna
Sim, sou de Wimbledon.
seem soh du wimbledon
Não, estou em negócios.
*nãhoo ee**shtoh** aheem nu**go**seeoosh*
Estou em Portugal por dois dias.
*ee**shtoh** aheem poortoo**gal** poor doheesh **dee**ahsh*

Getting Around.........

check out
1 false, on the left

2 false
3 7pm
4 yes, the taxi will take 10 minutes

lost for words

carro; autocarro; avião; moto; bicicleta; barco; metro; comboio

location, location, location

banco; castelo; praia; catedral; estação; largo; praça

as if you were there

Dois bilhetes de ida e volta para Óbidos, se faz favor.
*doheesh beell**eh**tush du **ee**dah ee **vol**tah **pah**rah **o**beedoosh su fash fah**vohr***
A que horas chega?
*a ku **o**rahsh **sheh**gah*
É directo?
*e dee**re**too*
Obrigada/o.
*obree**ga**dah/doo*

Somewhere to Stay.....

check out
1 double; how many nights?
2 €98
3 €165
4 €6

lost for words

across 5 televisão 6 cama
7 janela 9 zero
down 1 duche 2 carro 3 piscina
4 tenda 6 cofre 8 luz

match it up

1d 2a 3b 4e 5c

in the mix

1d noite 2e passaporte

3a elevador 4c problema
5b adultos

as if you were there

Queria pagar a conta.
*ku**ree**ah pah**gar** ah **kohñ**tah*
O número oito.
*oo **noo**muroo **ohee**too*
Quanto é?
***kwahñ**too e*
Em dinheiro.
*aheeḿ deeñn**yahee**roo*

Buying Things..........

check out

1 200 grammes
2 size 41; yes
3 €3

in the mix

1 cem gramas de queijo
2 uma garrafa de água mineral
3 meio quilo de presunto
4 um litro de vinho
5 um chouriço

opposites attract

1 pequeno 2 largo 3 caro

as if you were there

Queria exprimentar uns sapatos.
*ku**ree**ah aheeshpreemehn**tar**
oohnsh sah**pa**toosh*
O meu número é trinta e nove.
*oo **me**hoo **noo**muroo e **treen**tah
ee nov*
Fico com eles.
***fee**koo kohḿ **eh**lush*

Café Life...................

check out

1 no

2 what you want to drink
3 vanilla

in the mix

1 sumo de fruta 2 refrigerante
3 gelado 4 batido 5 tosta
6 garoto 7 prego 8 morango
9 sandes

downword

1 baunilha 2 troco 3 temos
4 sem 5 rissóis 6 tónico
7 sabores treat batatas fritas

as if you were there

Queria um gin-tónico.
*ku**ree**ah ooḿ geen**to**neekoo*
Sim. E um vinho branco.
*seeḿ. ee ooḿ **veeñ**nyoo
brahnkoo*
Queria acepipes variados,se faz
favor.
*ku**ree**ah ahsu**pee**push
vahree**a**doosh su fash fah**vohr***

Eating Out...............

check out

1 ten minutes; false, you are
  offered one near the window
2 chicken; a bottle of wine
3 true

question time

1a 2a 3b 4a 5b

match it up

mesa, lulas, tigela, sopa, carne,
molho

as if you were there

Sim, obrigado/a. Está muito bom.
*seeḿ obree**ga**doo/ah. ee**shta
mooeentoo bohḿ*

A conta, se faz favor.
*ah **kohn**tah su fash fah**vohr***
Aceita cartões de crédito?
*ah**saheet**ah kahrt**ōheesh** du **kre**deetoo*
Está incluído o serviço?
*ee**shta** eenkloo**ee**doo oo sur**vee**soo*
Obrigado/a. Adeus.
*obree**ga**doo/ah. ah**deh**oosh*

Entertainment...........

check out
1 from 10am to 7pm – nine hours
2 Saturday

lost for words

espectáculo, esquis, surf, exposição, vestiário, estádio, golfe, museu, vela, festa, visita, toalha, mesa

match it up

prancha de wind-surf; tacos de golfe; raqueta de ténis; barco à vela

in the mix

1 alpinismo 2 cinema
3 espreguiçadeira 4 galeria
5 esgotado 6 legendas
7 intervalo 8 plateia

as if you were there

Posso usar a piscina do hotel?
po**soo oo**zar** ah pee**shsee**nah doo o**tel
Queria alugar uma espreguiçadeira.
*ku**ree**ah ahloo**gar oo**mah eeshprugeesah**dahee**rah*

Sim, obrigado/a. Onde são os chuveiros?
*seem̃ obree**ga**doo/ah. ohnd sãhoo oosh shoo**vahee**roosh*

Emergencies............

check out
1 false, he says it's not serious
2 three times a day, with water, after meals
3 false, the clutch isn't working
4 this morning; fill in a form

question time

1 Há alguém aqui que fale inglês?
(Is there someone here who speaks English?)
2 Onde lhe dói?
(Where does it hurt?)
3 Tem aspirinas?
(Do you have any aspirin?)
4 Quando estará pronto?
(When will it be ready?)
5 Qual é o seu nome?
(What is your name?)

match it up

Chamo a polícia; Preciso duma ambulância; Queria uma consulta; Tenho tosse; Não posso mexer o dedo; Perdi o meu relógio.

as if you were there

Perdi um chumbo. Tenho dor de dentes.
*pur**dee** oom̃ **shoom**boo. ta**heenn**yoo dohr du **dehn**tush*
É grave?
e grav
Obrigado/a.
*obree**ga**doo/ahh*

(m) = masculine   (f) = feminine
(pl) = plural   (sing) = singular
Verbs that follow a regular pattern are
shown as (regular). For more on verb
endings see the Language Builder, p132.

A

a little (i.e. not much) um pouco *oom pohkoo*
accelerator acelerador, o *ahsulahrahdohr*
to accept aceitar *ahsaheetar*
adaptor adaptador, o *adaptahdohr*
address endereço, o *ehndurehsoo*
address morada, a *mooradah*
adult adulto, o *ahdooltoo*
after depois de *dupoheesh du*
afternoon/evening tarde, a *tard*
after-sun lotion loção pós-sol, a *loosãhoo posh-sol*
air ar, o *ar*
air conditioning ar condicionado, o *ar kohndeeseeoonadoo*
all, everything tudo *toodoo*
allergic alérgico/a *ahlerjeekoolah*
allowed permitido *purmeeteedoo*
almond amêndoa, a *ahmehndooah*
almond biscuits bolinhos de amêndoa, os *booleennyoosh du ahmehndooah*
always sempre *sehmpru*
ambulance ambulância, a *ahmboolahnseeah*
ankle tornozelo, o *toornuzehloo*
antibiotics antibióticos, os *ahnteebeeoteekoosh*
antique shop antiquário, o *ahnteekooareeoo*
anything else? mais alguma coisa? *maheesh algoomah koheezah*
aperitif aperitivo, o *ahpureeteevoo*
apple maçã, a *mahsãh*
to apply, put on aplicar *ahpleekar*
appointment (with doctor, dentist) consulta, a *kohnsooltah*
apricot alperce, o *alpers*
arm braço, o *brasoo*
arrival chegada, a *shugadah*
to arrive chegar *shugar*
art gallery galeria de arte, a *gahlureeah du art*
article artigo, o *ahrteegoo*
ashtray cinzeiro, o *seenzaheeroo*
asparagus espargos, os *eeshpargoosh*
aspirins aspirinas, as *ahshpeereenahsh*
aubergine berinjela, a *bureeñjelah*

B

baby bebé, o *bebe*
back costas, as *koshtahsh*

back, background fundo, o *foondoo*
bag bolsa, a *bohlsah*
bag saco, o *sakoo*
balcony varanda, a *varahndah*
banana banana, a *bahnahnah*
bank banco, o *bahñkoo*
bathing hut barraca, a *bahrrakah*
battery pilha, a *peellah*
to be (see p134) estar, ser *eeshtar, sehr*
  I am sou/estou *soh/eeshtoh*
  (it, he, she) is/(you) are é *e*
  (they, you) are são *sãhoo*
to be (situated)/remain ficar (regular) *feekar*
to be able, can poder *poodehr*
  I can posso *pos*
to be called chamar-se (regular) *shahmarsu*
beach praia, a *praeeah*
(green) beans feijões verdes, os/vagens, as *faheejõheesh vehrdush/vajahneesh*
bed cama, a *kahmah*
beer/lager cerveja, a *survaheejah*
before antes de *ahntush du*
to begin começar (regular) *koomusar*
behind atrás *ahtrash*
belt cinto, o *seeñtoo*
berries amoras, as *ahmorahsh*
bigger maior *maheeor*
bike bicicleta, a *beeseekletah*
bill conta, a *kohñtah*
bit bocado, o *bookadoo*
to bite morder (regular) *moordehr*
black preto/a *prehtoolah*
black coffee (very strong) bica, a *beekah*
blanket cobertor, o *kooburtohr*
blind (for window) estore, o *eeshtor*
blouse blusa, a *bloozah*
blue azul *ahzool*
boat barco, o *barkoo*
bone osso, o *ohsoo*
booklet of tickets caderneta, a *kadurnehtah*
bookseller's livraria, a *leevrareeah*
boots botas, as *botahsh*
bottle garrafa, a *gahrrafah*
bowl tigela, a *teejelah*
box (in theatre) camarote, o *kahmahrot*
boy rapaz, o *rrahpahsh*
bra soutien, o *sooteeãh*
brakes travões, os *trahvõheesh*
brandy aguardente, o *agooahahrdehnt*
bread pão, o *pãhoo*
bread roll pãozinho, o *pãhoozeennyoo*
bread rolls papos-secos, os *papoosh-sehkoo*

bread shop padaria, a *padahreeah*

breakdown (car) avaria, a *ahvahreeah*

breakfast pequeno almoço, o *pukehnoo almohsoo*

bridge ponte, a *pohnt*

briefcase pasta, a *pashtah*

to bring trazer *trahzehr*

broad beans favas, as *favahsh*

broken partido/a *pahrteedoo/ah*

brown castanho/a *kahshtahnnyoo/ah*

bullfight tourada, a *tohradah*

burn queimadura, a *kaheemahdoorah*

to burn queimar (regular) *kaheemar*

bus autocarro, o *aotokarroo*

business negócios, os *nugoseeoosh*

butcher's talho, o *talloo*

to buy comprar (regular) *kohmprar*

C

café (for cakes and pastries) confeitaria, a *kohnfaheetahreeah*

café (for a range of snacks) café, o *kahfe*

café (or shop for cakes and pastries) pastelaria, a *pahshtulahreeah*

caffeine cafeína, a *kafaheenah*

cake bolo, o *bohloo*

call chamada, a *shahmadah*

camera (digital) câmara (digital), a *kahmahrah (deejeetal)*

camera shop loja de artigos fotográficos, a *lojah du ahrteegoosh footoografeekoosh*

campsite parque de campismo, o *park du kahmpeeshmoo*

car carro, o *karroo*

car park parque de estacionamento, o *park du eeshtahseeoonahmehntoo*

caravan caravana, a *karahvahnah*

card, pass cartão, o *kahrtãoo*

carrot cenoura, a *sunohrah*

castle castelo, o *kahshteloo*

cathedral catedral, a *kahtudral*

cauliflower couve-flor, a *kohvu-flohr*

centre centro, o *sehntroo*

chair cadeira, a *kahdaheerah*

change troco, o *trohkoo*

to change mudar (regular), trocar (regular) *moodar, trookar*

to charge, collect cobrar (regular) *koobrar*

cheap barato/a *bahratoolah*

cheese queijo, o *kaheejoo*

cheesecake/cheese tart queijada, a *kaheejadah*

chemist's farmácia, a *fahrmaseeah*

cherry cereja, a *surahheejah*

chest peito, o *paheetoo*

chestnut castanha, a *kahshtahnnyah*

to chew mastigar (regular) *mahshteegar*

chickpeas grãos de bico, os *grähoosh du beecoo*

child criança, a *kreeahnsah*

chin queixo, o *kaheeshoo*

china louças de porcelana, as *lohsahsh du poorsulahnah*

chips batatas fritas, as *bahtatahsh freetahsh*

church igreja, a *eegraheejah*

cigarette cigarro, o *seegaroo*

cinema cinema, o *seenehmah*

circle (in theatre) balcão, o *balkähoo*

city/town cidade, a *seedad*

class classe, a *klas*

climbing alpinismo, o *alpeeneeshmoo*

cloakroom vestiário, o *vushteeareeoo*

to close fechar (regular) *fushar*

closed fechado/a *fushadoo/ah*

clothes roupa, a *rrohpah*

clothes shop loja de roupas, a *lojah du rrohpahsh*

clutch embriagem, a *ehmbreeajaheem*

coach camioneta, a *kahmeeoonetah*

(salted) cod bacalhau, o *bahkahllaoo*

coffee café, o *kahfe*

white coffee (small) garoto, o *gahrohtoo*

white coffee (large, milky) galão, o *gahlähoo*

cognac conhaque, o *konnyak*

cold constipação, a *kohnshteepahsähoo*

cold frio/a *freeoo/ah*

cold meat carnes frias, as *karnush freeahsh*

colour cor, a *kohr*

comb pente, o *pehnt*

commission comissão, a *koomeesähoo*

concert concerto, o *kohnsehrtoo*

concert hall sala de concertos, a *salah du kohnsehrtoosh*

connection ligação, a *leegahsähoo*

constipation prisão de ventre, a *preezähoo du vehntru*

contact lenses lentes de contacto, as *lehntush du kohntatoo*

to contain conter *kohntehr*

contraceptives contraceptivos, os *kohntraseteevoosh*

control contrôlo, o *kohntrohloo*

type of cooking pot cataplana, a *kahtahplahnah*

corner esquina, a *eeshkeenah*

correct certo/a *sertoolah*

to cost custar (regular) *kooshtar*
cough tosse, a *tos*
cough mixture xarope para a tosse, o *shahrop pahrah ah tos*
(married) couple casal, o *kahzal*
cream creme, o *krem*
credit card cartão de crédito, o *kahrtãhoo du kredeetoo*
to cross atravessar (regular) *ahtrahvusar*
cup chávena, a *shavunah*
curtain cortina, a *koorteenah*
custard tarts pastéis de Belém/nata, os *pahshteeesh du blaheem/natah*
customs alfândega, a *alfahndugah*
to cut cortar (regular) *koortar*

D

dairy leitaria, a *laheetahreeah*
danger perigo, o *pureegoo*
dark escuro/a *eeshkooroo/ah*
dates tâmaras, as *tahmahrahsh*
daughter filha, a *feellah*
day dia, o *deeah*
decaffeinated descafeinado *dushkahfaheenadoo*
deck chair cadeira de lona, a *kahdaheerah du lohnah*
to delay demorar (regular) *dumoorar*
dentist dentista, o/a *dehnteeshtah*
deodorant desodorizante, o *duzodooreezahnt*
to depart partir (regular) *pahrteer*
department store grande armazém, o *grahnd armahzaheem*
departure partida, a *pahrteedah*
deposit sinal, o *seenal*
safe-deposit box cofre, o/caixa forte, a *kofru/kaeeshah fort*
to desire, want desejar (regular) *duzujar*
destination destino, o *dushteenoo*
to develop (film) revelar (regular) *rruvular*
diabetic diabético/a *deeahbeteekoo/ah*
to dial marcar (regular) *mahrkar*
diarrhoea diarreia, a *deeahrraheeah*
diesel gasóleo, o *gazoleeoo*
dinghy/sailing boat barco à vela, o *barkoo a velah*
direct directo/a *deeretoo/ah*
dirty sujo/a *soojoo/ah*
discount desconto, o *dushkohntoo*
distractions, entertainment distracções, as *deeshtrasõheesh*
diversion desvio, o *dushveeoo*
to do, make fazer *fahzehr*
doctor médico/a, o/a *medeekoo/ah*
dog cão, o *kãhoo*
door, gate porta, a *portah*

double room quarto duplo, o *kwartoo dooploo*
downstairs em baixo *aheembaheeshoo*
draught beer imperial, a *eempureeal*
dress vestido, o *vushteedoo*
drink bebida, a *bubeedah*
to drink beber (regular) *bubehr*
driving licence carta de condução, a *kartah du kohndoosãhoo*
dry seco/a *sehkoo/ah*
dustbin caixote de lixo, o *kaheeshot du leeshoo*

E

(inner) ear ouvido, o *ohveedoo*
(outer) ear orelha, a *ohrehllah*
earthenware louças de barro, as *lohsahsh du barroo*
east (l)este, o *(l)ehsht*
to eat comer (regular) *koomehr*
elbow cotovelo, o *kootoovehloo*
(fried) egg ovo (estrelado), o *ohvoo (eeshtruladoo)*
embroidery bordados, os *boordadoosh*
end fim, o *feem*
to end, finish terminar (regular) *turmeenar*
engine (car) motor, o *mootohr*
enjoy your meal! bom apetite! *bohm ahputeet*
entrance entrada, a *ehntradah*
exactly exactamente *ehzatahmehnt*
to examine examinar (regular) *eezahmeenar*
exchange (rate) câmbio, o *kahmbeeoo*
excursion, trip excursão, a *aheeshkoorsãhoo*
excuse me (to get past) com licença *kohm leesehnsah*
excuse me! (to attract attention)/sorry desculpe *dushkoolp*
exercise exercício, o *ehzurseeseeoo*
exhibition exposição, a *aheeshpoozeesãhoo*
exit saída, a *saheedah*
expensive caro/a *karoo/ah*
eye olho, o *ohlloo*

F

face cara, a *karah*
family família, a *fahmeeleeah*
far longe *lonj*
fashion moda, a *modah*
to feel sentir-se *sehnteer-su*
ferry ferry-boat, o *fereeboht*
fever febre, a *febr*
fiesta/celebration/party festa, a *feshtah*
fig figo, o *feegoo*

filigree jewellery filigranas, as *feeleegrahnahsh*

to fill encher (regular) *ehnshehr*

to fill in preencher (regular) *preeehnshehr*

filling (at dentist's) chumbo, o *shoomboo*

film filme, o *feelm*

roll of film rolo, o *rrohloo*

to find encontrar (regular) *ehnkohntrar*

fingers dedos, os *dehdoosh*

to finish acabar (regular) *ahkahbar*

fireworks fogos de artifício, os *fogoosh du ahrteefeeseeoo*

first primeiro/a *preemaheerooloah*

fish peixe, o *paheesh*

fishmonger's peixaria, a *paheeshahreeah*

fitness centre, gym ginásio, o *jeenazeeoo*

fitting room provador, o *proovahdohr*

flat tyre pneu furado, o *pnehoo fooradoo*

flat, apartment apartamento, o *ahpahrtahmehntoo*

flavour sabor, o *sahbohr*

flight voo, o *vohoo*

floor, storey andar, o *ahndar*

florist's florista, a *flooreeshtah*

flour farinha, a *fahreennyah*

food comida, a *koomeedah*

food shop/grocer's mercearia, a *murseeahreeah*

foot pé, o *pe*

football futebol, o *footubol*

for, towards para *pahrah*

for/by/per/along por *poor*

for how long? por quanto tempo? *poor kwañtoo tehmpoo*

forbidden proibido *prooeebeedoo*

forehead testa, a *teshtah*

fork garfo, o *garfoo*

form ficha, a/ impresso, o *feeshah/ eempresoo*

four-star (petrol) super, o *sooper*

free, available livre *leevr*

free, unoccupied vago/a *vagooloah*

from/of de *du*

fruit fruta, a *frootah*

full cheio/a *shaheeooloah*

full board pensão completa, a *pehnsãhoo kohmpletah*

funicular/lift elevador, o *eeluvahdohr*

G

game, match jogo, o *johgoo*

garage garagem, a *gahrajaheeñ*

garden jardim, o *jahrdeeñ*

garlic alho, o *alloo*

gate portão, o *poortãhoo*

to get off, go down descer *dushsehr*

to get up levantar-se (regular) *luvahntarsu*

get undressed dispa-se *deeshpahsu*

gin and tonic gin-tónico, o *jeentoneekoo*

girl rapariga, a *rrahpahreega*

to give dar *dar*

glass copo, o *kopoo*

gloves luvas, as *loovahsh*

to go ir *eer*

I go, am going vou *voh*

(he, she) goes/(you) go vai *vaee*

golf golfe, o *golf*

golf clubs tacos de golfe, os *takoosh du golf*

golf course campo de golfe, o *kahmpoo du golf*

good bom, boa *bohñ, bohah*

good afternoon/evening boa tarde *bohah tard*

goodbye adeus *ahdehoosh*

good morning bom dia *bohm deeah*

good night boa noite *bohah noheet*

gramme grama, o *grahmah*

grapefruit toranja, a *toorahnjah*

grapes uvas, as *oovahsh*

green verde *vehrd*

grey cinzento/a *seenzehntooloah*

grilled grelhado/a *grulladooloah*

ground floor rés-do-chão, o *rresh-doo-shãhoo*

guesthouse pensão, a/residencial, o *pehnsãhoo/rruzeedehnseeal*

guidebook guia, o *geeah*

guided guiado/a *geeadooloah*

H

hair cabelo, o *kahbehloo*

hairdryer secador de cabelo, o *sukahdohr du kahbehloo*

hairdresser's cabeleireiro, o *kahbulaheeraheeroo*

half meio/a *maheeooloah*

half board meia pensão *maheeah pehnsãhoo*

ham fiambre, o/presunto, o *feeahmbr/ pruzoontoo*

hand mão, a *mãhoo*

handbag bolsa de mão, a/saco de mão, o *bohlsah du mahoo/sakoo du mãhoo*

handkerchiefs lenços, os *lehnsoosh*

handle puxador, o *poosahdohr*

to happen acontecer *ahkohntusehr*

hardware store loja de ferragens, a *lojah du furrajaheensh*
hat chapéu, o *shahpeoo*
to have ter *tehr*
  I have tenho *taheennyoo*
  (we) have temos *tehmoosh*
  (you) have/(he/she/it) has tem *taheeem*
to have to, must dever (regular) *duvehr*
hazelnut avelã, a *ahvulãh*
head cabeça, a *kahbehsah*
headlights faróis, os *fahroeesh*
health saúde, a *sahood*
health food shop loja de produtos dietéticos, a *lojah du proodootoosh deeuteteekoosh*
heel calcanhar, o *kalkahnnnyar*
hello! olá! *ola*
help! socorro! *sohkohrroo*
to help ajudar (regular) *ahjoodar*
her, it/she ela *elah*
here aqui *ahkee*
him, it/he ele *ehl*
hip anca, a *ahnkah*
hired, rented alugado/a *ahloogadoo/ah*
to hire alugar (regular) *ahloogar*
holidays férias, as *fereeahsh*
honey mel, o *mel*
hors d'œuvres acepipes variados, os *ahsupeepush vahreeadoosh*
horseriding equitação, a *ehkeetahsãhoo*
hostel casa de hóspedes, a/hospedaria, a *kazah du oshpudush/oshpudahreeah*
hot quente *kehnt*
hot dog cachorro (quente), o *kahshohrroo (kehnt)*
hotel hotel, o *otel*
  up-market hotel pousada, a *pohzadah*
how? como? *kohmoo*
how much? quanto? *kwahñtoo*
hundred (see p15) cem, cento *sehm, sehntoo*
to hurt doer *dooehr*
  (it) hurts dói *doee*
  (they) hurt doem *doaheeem*
hydrofoil hidroplano, o *eedroplahnoo*

I

ice gelo, o *jehloo*
ice cold/cool fresco/a *frehshkoo/ah*
in em *aheeem*
  in the (plural) nos, nas *noosh, nahsh*
  in the (singular) no, na *noo, nah*
  in one hour daqui a uma hora *dahkee ah oomah orah*
included incluído/a *eenklooeedoo/ah*
to include incluir *eenklooeer*
to inform, advise avisar (regular) *ahveezar*

information informações, as *eenfoormahsõheesh*
inn albergaria, a/estalagem, a *alburgahreeah/eeshtahlajaheeem*
insect insecto, o *eensetoo*
insurance seguro, o *sugooroo*
interested interessado/a *eenturusadoo/a*
interval intervalo, o *eenturvaloo*
iron ferro, o *ferroo*
it doesn't matter (either way) tanto faz *tahnto fash*

J

jacket casaco, o *kahzakoo*
jar frasco, o *frashkoo*
jeweller's joalharia, a *jooahllahreeah*
jewellery jóias, as *joeeahsh*
jug, carafe jarro, o *jarroo*
juice sumo, o *soomoo*

K

kale couve portuguesa, a *kohv poortoogehzah*
keep, stay mantenha-se *mahntaheenhahsu*
to keep guardar (regular) *gooahrdar*
key chave, a *shav*
kidneys rins, os *rreensh*
kilo quilo, o *keeloo*
kilometre quilómetro, o *keelomutroo*
knee joelho, o *jooehlloo*
knife faca, a *fakah*
to know (something) saber *sahbehr*
  I know sei *sahee*
to know (a person or place) conhecer *koonnyusehr*

L

lacework rendas, as *rrehndahsh*
lamp lâmpada, a *lahmpahdah*
large grande *grahnd*
laptop computador portátil, o *kohmpootahdohr poortateel*
to last durar (regular) *doorar*
late tarde *tard*
later mais tarde *maheesh tard*
laundrette (dry cleaner's) lavandaria (a seco), a *lahvahndahreeah (ah sehkoo)*
leather couro, o/ pele, a *kohroo/pel*
to leave deixar (regular) *daheeshar*
left esquerda, a *eeshkehrdah*
left-luggage depósito de bagagens, o *dupozeetoo do bahgajaheensh*
leg perna, a *pernah*
lemon limão, o *leemãhoo*
lemonade limonada, a *leemoonadah*
lentils lentilhas, as *lehnteellahsh*
lesson lição, a *leesãhoo*
letter carta, a *kartah*

lettuce alface, a *alfas*
to lie down deitar-se (regular)
  daheetarsu
life-belt, life-ring cinto de salvação, o
  seentoo du salvahsãhoo
lifeguard salva-vidas, o/a *salvah
  veedahsh*
lift ascensor, o *ahshsehnsohr*
light (weight) leve *lev*
light (-coloured) claro/a *klaroo/ah*
to light up acender (regular)
  ahsehndehr
to like gostar de (regular) *gooshtar du*
  I like it, him/her gosto dele/a
  goshtoo dehl/ah
  I like them gosto deles/as *goshtoo
  dehlush/dehlahsh*
like this, thus assim *ahseem*
line, track, platform linha, a *leennyah*
lips lábios, os *labeeoosh*
liquid líquido, o *leekeedoo*
list lista, a *leeshtah*
to live in morar em (regular) *moorar
  aheem*
liver fígado, o *feegahdoo*
to look olhar (regular) *ollar*
to look for buscar (regular) *booshkar*
to lose perder *purdehr*
lost property perdidos e achados
  purdeedoosh ee ahshadoosh
lotion loção, a *loosãhoo*
luggage bagagem, a *bahgajaheem*

M

magazine revista, a *rruveeshtah*
to make a mistake enganar-se
  (regular) *ehngahnarsu*
man homem, o *omaheem*
map, plan (of town) mapa, o/planta, a
  mapah/plahntah
market mercado, o *murkadoo*
market/funfair feira, a *faheerah*
married casado/a *kahzadoo/ah*
matches fósforos, os *foshfuroosh*
meal refeição, a *rrufaheesãhoo*
meat carne, a *karn*
medicine medicamento, o
  mudeekahmehntoo
medium médio/a *medeeoo/ah*
meeting room sala de reunião, a *salah
  du rrehooneeãhoo*
melon melão, o *mulãhoo*
memory card cartão memória, o
  kahrtãhoo mumoreeah
menu ementa, a *eemehntah*
milk leite, o *laheet*
milkshake batido, o *bahteedoo*

mineral water água mineral, a *agooah
  meenural*
mobile phone telemóvel, o *telemovel*
money dinheiro, o *deennyaheeroo*
more mais *maheesh*
mosque mesquita, a *mushkeetah*
motorbike motocicleta, a
  motoseekletah
motorway auto-estrada, a *aooto-
  eeshtradah*
mouth boca, a *bohkah*
to move mexer (regular) *mushehr*
mp3 player leitor de mp3, o *laheetohr
  du em peh trehsh*
much/many muito/a/os/as
  mooeentoo/ah/oosh/ahsh
museum museu, o *moozehoo*
mushroom cogumelo, o *koogoomeloo*
my meu, o (m) minha, a (f) *mehoo,
  meennyah*

N

nails unhas, as *oonnyahsh*
name nome, o *nohm*
  my name is chamo-me *shahmoomu*
napkin guardanapo, o
  gooahrdahnapoo
nappies fraldas, as *fraldahsh*
narrow estreito/a *eeshtraheetoo/ah*
nausea náuseas, as *naoozeeahsh*
near (here) perto daqui *pertoo
  (dahkee)*
neck pescoço, o *pushkohsoo*
necklace colar, o *koolar*
to need precisar de (regular)
  pruseezar du
newspaper jornal, o *joornal*
news-stand quiosque de jornais, o
  keeoshk du joornaeesh
next próximo/a *proseemoo/ah*
  next to ao pé de *aoo pe du*
  next to, beside ao lado de *aoo ladoo
  du*
  next, later depois *dupoheesh*
nice to meet you muito prazer
  mooeentoo prahzehr
night noite, a *noheet*
nightclub boîte, a *booat*
no access sentido proibido *sehnteedoo
  prooeebeedoo*
no through road sem saída *saheem
  saheedah*
no, not não *nãhoo*
north norte, o *nort*
nose nariz, o *nahreesh*
not yet ainda não *aheendah nãhoo*
nothing nada *nadah*
now agora *ahgorah*

number, size número, o *noomuroo*
numbered numerado/a *noomuradoo/ah*
nurse enfermeiro/a, o/a
 ehnfurmaheeroo/ah

O

occupied, taken ocupado/a *okoopadoo/ah*
of the (pl) dos, das *doosh, dahsh*
of the (sing) do, da *doo, dah*
oil óleo, o *oleeoo*
oil (olive) azeite, o *ahzaheet*
olives azeitonas, as *ahzaheetohnahsh*
once, one time uma vez *oomah vehsh*
onion cebola, a *subohlah*
only só *so*
open aberto/a *ahbertoo/ah*
to open abrir (regular) *ahbreer*
operation operação, a *opurahsãhoo*
opposite em frente *aheemfrehnt*
optician oculista, o *okooleeshtah*
orange (colour) cor-de-laranja *kohr-du-lahranjah*
orange laranja, a *lahranjah*
orangeade laranjada, a *lahrahnjadah*
to order encomendar (regular)
 ehnkohmehndar
to order, ask for pedir *pudeer*
outside fora *forah*
outside call (telephone) ligação exterior,
 a *leegahsãhoo aheeshtureeohr*

P

packet pacote, o *pahkot*
pain dor, a *dohr*
paper papel, o *pahpel*
parasol guarda-sol, o/chapéu de sol, o
 gooardah-sol/shapeoo du sol
pardon? como disse? *kohmoo dees*
park parque, o *park*
to park estacionar (regular)
 eeshtahseeoonar
parking estacionamento, o
 eeshtahseeoonahmehntoo
parsley salsa, a *salsah*
part (of car) peça, a *pesah*
passport passaporte, o *pasahport*
to pay (for) pagar (regular) *pahgar*
payment in advance pré-pagamento
 pre-pahgahmehntoo
peace paz, a *pash*
peach pêssego, o *pehsugoo*
peanut amendoin, o *ahmehndooeem*
pear pêra, a *pehrah*
pedestrians peões, os *peeõheesh*
pencil lápis, o *lapeesh*
pepper (vegetable) pimento, o
 peemehntoo
pepper (seasoning) pimenta, a
 peemehntah

person pessoa, a *pusohah*
petrol gasolina, a *gahzooleenah*
photo(graph), print foto(grafia), a
 footoo(grahfeeah)
pillow almofada, a *almoofadah*
pillow case fronha, a *frohnnyah*
pills, tablets comprimidos, os
 kohmpreemeedoosh
pineapple ananás, o *ahnahnash*
pink cor-de-rosa *kohr-du-rrozah*
pistachio pistacho, o *peeshtashoo*
place, site lugar, o *oo loogar*
plane avião, o *ahveeãhoo*
plasters adesivos, os *ahduzeevoosh*
plate, dish/course prato, o *pratoo*
platform cais, o *kaeesh*
to play (sport) jogar (regular) *joogar*
please se faz favor, por favor *su fash
 fahvohr, poor fahvohr*
plug (socket) tomada, a *toomadah*
plum ameixa, a *ahmaheeshah*
police polícia, a *pooleeseeah*
police station esquadra de polícia, a
 eeshkwadrah du pooleeseeah
port (wine) (vinho do) Porto, o
 veennyoo doo pohrtoo
portion dose, a *doz*
Portuguese português/esa
 poortoogehsh/ehzah
post office, post correio, o *koorraheeoo*
postcard postal, o *pooshtal*
potato batata, a *bahtatah*
pound sterling libra esterlina, a *leebrah
 eeshturleenah*
prawn gamba, a *gahmbah*
pregnant grávida *graveedah*
prescription receita, a *rrusaheetah*
price preço, o *prehsoo*
priority prioridade, a *preeooreedad*
to print imprimir (regular) *eempreemee...*
problem problema, o *prooblehmah*
programme programa, o *proograhmah*
pudding, dessert sobremesa, a
 soobrumehzah
to pull out, take out tirar (regular) *teera...*
pullover pulôver, o *poolohver*
to punch (ticket) obliterar (regular)
 obleeturar
purple púrpura *poorpoorah*
to put (in) meter (regular) *mutehr*

Q

quite, fairly bastante *bahshtahnt*

R

racket raqueta, a *rraketah*
radiator radiador, o *rradeeahdohr*
radio rádio, o *rradeeoo*

railway caminho de ferro, o *kahmeennyoo du ferroo*
raincoat impermeável, o *eempurmeeavel*
raspberry framboesa, a *frahmbooehzah*
razor blades lâminas de barbear, as *lahmeenahsh du bahrbeear*
ready pronto *prohntoo*
receipt recibo, o *ruseeboo*
to recommend recomendar (regular) *rrukoomehndar*
red vermelho/a *vurmehlloo/ah*
red wine vinho tinto, o *veennyoo teentoo*
to reduce reduzir (regular) *rrudoozeer*
region região, a *rrugeeãhoo*
registration number (of car) matrícula, a *mahtreekoolah*
to repeat repetir *rruputeer*
to reserve reservar (regular) *rruzurvar*
I have a reservation mandei reservar *mahndahee rruzurvar*
reserved reservado/a *rruzurvadoo/ah*
to rest descansar (regular) *dushkahnsar*
restaurant restaurante, o *rrushtaoorahnt*
restaurant (playing fado music) casa de fados, a *kazah du fadoosh*
retired reformado/a *rrufoormadoo/ah*
to return regressar (regular), voltar (regular) *rrugrusar, voltar*
right direita, a *deeraheetah*
road estrada, a *eeshtradah*
roadworks obras, as *obrahsh*
room/quarter quarto, o *kwartoo*
single room quarto individual, o *kwartoo eendeeveedooal*
room to let dormida, a *doormeedah*
rug tapete, o *tahpeht*
to run correr (regular) *koorrehr*

S

sachet pacotinho, o *pahkooteennyoo*
safe cofre, o *kofr*
sailing/sail vela, a *velah*
salad salada, a *sahladah*
salt sal, o *sal*
sandals sandálias, as *sahndaleeahsh*
sanitary towels pensos higiénicos, os/ toalhas absorventes, as *pehnsoosh eejeeeneekoosh/tooallahsh ahbusorvehntush*
sardines sardinhas, as *sahrdeennyahsh*
sauce molho, o *mohlloo*
saucer pires, o *peerush*
sauna sauna, a *saoonah*

to say, tell dizer *deezehr*
scarf cachecol, o *kashkol*
school escola, a *eeshkolah*
second segundo/a *sugoondoo/ah*
section, department secção, a *seksãhoo*
security segurança, a *sugoorahnsah*
to see ver *vehr*
to send mandar (regular) *mahndar*
serious grave *grav*
service serviço, o *surveesoo*
several vários/as *vareeoosh/ahsh*
shawl xaile, o *shaeel*
shellfish, seafood mariscos, os *mahreeshkoosh*
shellfish and seafood restaurant marisqueira, a *mahreeshkaheerah*
shirt camisa, a *kahmeezah*
shoes sapatos, os *sahpatoosh*
shoe shop sapataria, a *sahpahtahreeah*
shop loja, a *lojah*
shopping area zona comercial, a *zohnah koomurseeal*
shopping centre centro comercial, o *sehntroo koomurseeal*
shorts calções, os *kalsõheesh*
shoulder ombro, o *ohmbroo*
show espectáculo, o *eeshpetakooloo*
shower duche, o/chuveiro, o *doosh/shoovaheeroo*
shrimps camarões, os *kahmahrõheesh*
to sign assinar (regular) *ahseenar*
single/simple simples *seemplush*
single (not married) solteiro/a *soltaheeroo/ah*
sink lavatório, o *lahvahtoreeoo*
to sit down sentar-se (regular) *sehntarsu*
skirt saia, a *saheeah*
to sleep dormir *doormeer*
slice fatia, a *fahteeah*
slowly devagar *duvahgar*
small pequeno/a *pukehnoo/ah*
to smoke fumar (regular) *foomar*
smoker fumador, o *foomahdohr*
soap sabonete, o *sahbooneht*
socks peúgas, as *peeoogahsh*
soft drink refrigerante, o *rrufreejurahnt*
sold out esgotado/a *eeshgootadoo/ah*
some uns, umas *oonsh, oomahsh*
somebody alguém *algaheem*
something alguma coisa *algoomah koheezah*
son filho, o *feelloo*
I'm sorry lamento *lahmehntoo*
south sul, o *sool*

souvenir shop loja de lembranças, a *lojah du lehn**brahn**sahsh*

sparkling (mineral water) com gás *kohm gash*

to speak falar (regular) *fahlar*

speciality especialidade, a *eeshpuseeah**lee**dad*

speed velocidade, a *vuloosee**dad**

spicy sausage chouriço, o *shoh**ree**soo*

spoon colher, a *koo**ller***

sports shop loja de artigos desportivos, a *lojah du ahr**tee**goosh dushpoor**tee**voosh*

square largo, o *largoo*

square, market praça, a *prasah*

squid lula, a *loolah*

stadium estádio, o *eesh**ta**deeoo*

stairs escada, a *eesh**ka**dah*

stalls (in theatre) plateia, a *plahta**hee**ah*

stamp selo, o *sehloo*

to stamp (ticket) carimbar (regular) *kahreem**bar***

station estação, a *eeshtah**sã**hoo*

stationer's papelaria, a *pahpulah**ree**ah*

steak bife, a *beef*

steak sandwich prego, o *pregoo*

to steal, rob roubar (regular) *rrohbar*

steering wheel volante, o *voo**lahnt***

steering/address direcção, a *deere**sã**hoo*

still (mineral water) sem gás *saheem gash*

sting picada, a *pee**ka**dah*

to sting picar (regular) *pee**kar***

stomach estômago, o *eesh**toh**mahgoo*

stop paragem, a *pahra**jaheem***

to stop parar (regular) *pahrar*

straight on sempre em frente *sehmpr aheem frehnt*

strawberry morango, o *moo**rahn**goo*

street rua, a *rrooah*

student estudante, o/a *eeshtoo**dahnt***

stuffed recheado/a *rrushee**a**doo**lah*

subtitles legendas, as *lu**jehn**dahsh*

to suffer sofrer (regular) *soo**frehr***

sugar açúcar, o *ah**soo**kar*

suitcase mala, a *malah*

to sunbathe bronzear (regular) *brohnzee**ar***

sunbed, lounger espreguiçadeira, a *eeshpruguee**sah**da**hee**rah*

sunburn queimadura solar, a *keheema**doo**rah soh**lar***

sun cream creme para bronzear, o *krem pahrah brohnzee**ar***

sunglasses óculos de sol, os *o**koo**loosh du sol*

sunstroke insolação, a *eensoolah**sã**hoo*

supermarket supermercado, o *soopermur**ka**doo*

supplement suplemento, o *sooplu**mehn**too*

surfboard prancha de surf, a *prahnshah du surf*

surfing surf, o *surf*

to swallow engolir (regular) *ehngoo**leer***

sweater camisola, a *kahmee**zo**lah*

sweet doce *dohs*

sweets rebuçados, os *rruboo**sa**doosh*

to swim nadar (regular) *nahdar*

swimming costume fato de banho, o *fatoo du bah**ññ**yoo*

swimming pool piscina, a *peesh**see**nah*

T

table mesa, a *mehzah*

tablecloth toalha de mesa, a *too**a**llah du mehzah*

to take photos tirar fotografias (regular) *teerar footoograh**fee**ahsh*

to take, have tomar (regular) *toomar*

tap torneira, a *toorna**hee**rah*

tavern tasca, a *tashkah*

taxi rank praça de táxis, a *prasah du takseesh*

tea chá, o *sha*

tea room salão de chá, o *sah**lã**hoo du sha*

teaspoon colher de chá, a *koo**ller** du sha*

telephone telefone, o *tulufon*

telephone card cartão de telefone, o *kahr**tã**hoo du tulufon*

television televisão, a *tuluvee**zã**hoo*

room temperature natural *nah**too**ral*

temple templo, o *tehmploo*

temporary provisório/a *proovee**zo**reeoo**la**

tennis ténis, o *teneesh*

tennis balls bolas de ténis, as *bolahsh du teneesh*

tennis court campo de ténis, o *kahmpoo du teneesh*

tent tenda, a *tehndah*

terrace terraço, o *turrasoo*

thank you obrigado/a *obreega**do**lah*

that aquele/aquela *ah**kel**/ah**ke**lah*

that (neutral) isso/aquilo *eesoo/ah**kee**loo*

the o (m) os (mpl) *oo, oosh*

the a (f) as (fpl) *ah, ahsh*

theatre teatro, o *teea**troo**

their(s) seus (m)/suas (f) *seh**oosh**/sooahsh*

then, next logo *logoo*

there aí, lá *ahee, la*

there is/are há *ha*

these estes/estas *ehsh**tush**/esh**tahsh*

thigh coxa, a *kohshah*

to think (express belief) crer *krehr*

I think creio *kra**hee**o*

148

to think pensar (regular) *pehnsar*
this este/esta *ehsht/ eshtah*
this (neutral) isto *eeshtoo*
throat garganta, a *gahrgahntah*
ticket bilhete, o *beelleht*
return ticket bilhete de ida e volta, o *beelleht du eedah ee voltah*
ticket office bilheteira, a *beellutaheerah*
tie gravata, a *grahvatah*
tights collant, o *kolahñ*
tile azulejo, o *ahzoolaheejoo*
till, cash desk caixa, a *kaeeshah*
tin, can lata, a *latah*
tissues lenços de papel, os *lehnsoosh du pahpel*
titbits, snacks petiscos, os *puteeshkoosh*
to a *ah*
toast (piece of) torrada, a *toorradah*
toasted sandwich tosta, a *toshtah*
tobacconist's tabacaria, a *tahbahkahreeah*
today hoje *ohj*
toes dedos do pé, os *dehdoosh doo pe*
toilet retrete, o *rrutret*
toilet, bathroom casa de banho, a *kazah du bahñnyoo*
toilets lavabos, os/sanitários, os *lahvaboosh/sahneetareeoosh*
toilet paper papel higiénico, o *pahpel eejeeeneekoo*
toll peagem, a/portagem, a *peeajaheeñ/poortajaheeñ*
tomato tomate, o *toomat*
tomorrow amanhã *amahnnyāh*
tooth dente, o *dehnt*
toothbrush escova de dentes, a *eeshkohvah du dehntush*
toothpaste pasta de dentes, a *pashtah du dehntush*
toothpicks palitos, os *pahleetoosh*
Tourist Office posto de turismo, o *pohshtoo du tooreeshmoo*
tourist pass/ticket bilhete turístico, o *beelleht tooreeshteekoo*
towel toalha, a *tooallah*
town vila, a *veelah*
toy shop loja de brinquedos, a *lojah du breenkehdoosh*
tracksuit fato de treino, o *fatoo du traheenoo*
train comboio, o *kohmboeeoo*
tram eléctrico, o *eeletreekoo*
trouser press passadeira (de calças), a *pahsahdaheerah (du kalsahsh)*
trousers calças, as *kalsahsh*

to try (on) experimentar (regular), provar (regular) *aheeshpureemehntar, proovar*
T-shirt T-shirt, a *teeshurt*
to turn virar (regular) *veerar*
twice, two times duas vezes *dooahsh vehzush*
type tipo, o *teepoo*
tyre pneu, o *pnehoo*

U

underdone (meat) mal passado/a *mal pahsadoo/ah*
underground/metre metro, o *metroo*
underpants cuecas, as *kooekahsh*
to understand compreender (regular) *kohmpreeendehr*
to undress despir *dushpeer*
unleaded sem chumbo *saheeñ shoomboo*
until/as far as até a *ahte ah*
upstairs em cima *aheeñseemah*
urgent urgente *oorjehnt*
to use usar (regular) *oozar*

V

vanilla baunilha, a *baooneellah*
VAT IVA, o *eevah*
vegetarian vegetariano/a *vujutahreeahnoo/ah*
very muito *mooeentoo*
view vista, a *veeshtah*
vinegar vinagre, o *veenagr*
visit visita, a *veezeetah*
volleyball voleibol, o *volaheebol*
to vomit vomitar (regular) *voomeetar*

W

to wait (for) esperar (regular) *eeshpurar*
waiting room sala de espera, a *salah du eeshperah*
to wake up acordar (regular) *ahkoordar*
wallet/purse carteira, a *kahrtaheerah*
walking, on foot a pé *ah pe*
walnuts nozes, as *nozush*
to want querer *kurehr*
  I would like queria *kureeah*
washing-up liquid detergente para a louça, o *duturjehnt pahrah ah lohsah*
watch relógio, o *rrulojeeoo*
water água, a *agooah*
watermelon melancia, a *mulahnseeah*
waterskiing/waterski esqui aquático, o *eeshkee ahkooateekoo*
way, road caminho, o *kahmeennyoo*
week semana, a *sumahnah*

weekdays dias úteis, os *dee*ahsh *oo*taheesh

well bem *baheem*

west oeste, o *oesht*

what que *ku*

  what time is it? que horas são? *ku* *o*rahsh *sah*oo

wheel roda, a *rro*dah

when quando *kwahñdoo*

where onde *ohnd*

whisky uísque, o *ooeeshk*

white branco/a *brahñkoo/ah*

who, whom quem *kaheem*

wickerwork artigos de verga, os *ahrteegoosh du vehrgah*

wide, broad largo/a *largoo/ah*

widow viúva, a *veeoo*vah

widower viúvo, o *veeoo*voo

window janela, a *jah*nelah

windscreen wiper limpador de pára-brisas, o *leempah***dohr** *du* *pa*rah-*bree*zahsh

windsurf board prancha à vela/de wind-surf, a *prahn*shah a *ve*lah/du *weend***surf**

windsurfing wind-surf, o *weend***surf**

wine vinho, o *veen*nyoo

wine merchant's comerciante de vinhos, o *koo*mursee**ahnt** *du* *veen*nyoosh

to wish, want querer (regular) *ku*rehr

with com *kohm*

without sem *saheem*

woman mulher, a *moo***ller**

wood madeira, a *mah***dahee**rah

to work trabalhar (regular) *trah*bah**llar**

to work, function funcionar (regular) *foon*seeoo**nar**

wrist pulso, o *pool*soo

Y

yellow amarelo/a *ah*mah**re**loo/ah

yes sim *seem*

yesterday ontem *ohn*taheem

you (f, very formal)/woman, lady senhora, a *sun***nyoh**rah

you (fairly polite, see p132) você *vo*seh

you (m, very formal)/man, gentleman senhor, o *sun***nyohr**

you're welcome não tem de quê *nah*hoo *ta*heem *du keh*

your/his/its seu, o (m) *seh*oo

your/her/its sua, a (f) *soo*ah

youth hostel pousada de juventude, a *poh***za**dah du joovehn**too**d

Z

zone, area zona, a *zoh*nah

a to
a, as the (f)
a pé on foot, walking
aberto/a open
abrir to open
acabar to finish
aceitar to accept
acelerador, o accelerator
acender to light up
acepipes variados, os hors d'œuvres
acontecer to happen
acordar to wake up
açúcar, o sugar
adaptador, o adaptor
adesivos, os plasters
adeus good bye
adulto, o adult
agora now
água, a water
água mineral, a mineral water
aguardente, o brandy
aí there
ainda não not yet
aipo, o celery
ajudar to help
albergaria, a inn
alérgico/a allergic
alface, a lettuce
alfândega, a customs
alguém somebody
alguma coisa something
alho, o garlic
almofada, a pillow
alperce, o apricot
alpinismo, o climbing
alugado/a hired, rented
alugar to hire
amanhã tomorrow
amarelo/a yellow
ambulância, a ambulance
ameixa, a plum
amêndoa, a almond
amendoim, o peanut
amoras, as berries
ananás, o pineapple
anca, a hip
andar, o floor, storey
antes de before
antibióticos, os antibiotics
antiquário, o antique shop
ao lado de next to, beside
ao pé de next to
apartamento, o flat, apartment
aperitivo, o aperitif
aplicar to apply, put on
aquele/a that

aqui here
ar, o air
ar condicionado, o air conditioning
artigo, o article
artigos de verga, os wickerwork
ascensor, o lift
aspirinas, as aspirins
assim like this, thus
assinar to sign
até a until/as far as
atrás behind
atravessar to cross
auto-estrada, a motorway
autocarro, o bus
avaria, a (car) breakdown
avelã, a hazelnut
avião, o plane
avisar to inform, advise
azeite, o oil
azeitonas, as olives
azul blue
azulejo, o tile

B

bacalhau, o salted cod
bagagem, a luggage
balcão, o circle (in theatre)
banana, a banana
banco, o bank
barato/a cheap
barco, o boat
barco à vela, o dinghy/sailing boat
barraca, a bathing hut
bastante quite, fairly
batata, a potato
batatas fritas, as chips
batido, o milk shake
baunilha, a vanilla
bebé, o baby
beber to drink
bebida, a drink
bem well
berinjela, a aubergine
bica, a black coffee (very strong)
bicicleta, a bike
bifana, a pork roll
bife, o steak
bilhete, o ticket
bilhete de ida e volta, o return ticket
bilhete turístico, o tourist pass/ticket
bilhetes combinados tickets for
    underground and bus
bilheteira, a ticket office
blusa, a blouse
boa noite good night
boa tarde good afternoon/evening
boca, a mouth
bocado, o bit

boîte, a nightclub
bolas de ténis, as tennis balls
bolinhos de amêndoa, os almond biscuits
bolo, o cake
bolsa, a bag
bolsa de mão, a handbag
bom apetite! enjoy your meal!
bom, boa good
bom dia good morning
bombeiros,os firemen
bordados, os embroidery
botas, as boots
braço, o arm
branco/a white
bronzear to sunbathe
buscar to look for

C

cabeça, a head
cabeleireiro, o hairdresser's
cabelo, o hair
cachecol, o scarf
cachorro (quente), o hot dog
cadeira, a chair
cadeira de lona, a deck chair
caderneta, a booklet of tickets
café, o café (for a larger range of snacks)/coffee
cafeína, a caffeine
cais, o platform
caixa, a till, cash desk
caixa forte, a safe-deposit box
caixote de lixo, o dustbin
calcanhar, o heel
calças, as trousers
calções, os shorts
cama, a bed
camarões, os shrimps
camarote, o box (in theatre)
câmbio, o exchange (rate)
caminho, o way, road
caminho de ferro, o railway
camioneta, a coach
camisa, a shirt
camisola, a sweater
campo de golfe, o golf course
campo de ténis, o tennis court
caneta, a pen
cão, o dog
cara, a face
carapau, o horse-mackerel
caravana, a caravan
carne, a meat
carnes frias, as cold meat
caril, o curry
caro/a expensive, dear
carro, o car
carta, a letter

carta de condução, a driving licence
cartão, o card, pass
cartão de crédito, o credit card
cartão de telefone, o telephone card
cartão memória, o memory card
carteira, a wallet/purse
casa de banho, a toilet, bathroom
casa de fados, a restaurant playing fado music
casa de hóspedes, a hostel
casaco, o jacket
casado/a married
casal, o (married) couple
castanha, a chestnut
castanho/a brown
castelo, o castle
cataplana, a type of cooking pot
catedral, a cathedral
cebola, a onion
cem hundred (see 15)
cenoura, a carrot
cento hundred (see p15)
centro, o centre
centro comercial, o shopping centre
cereja, a cherry
certo/a correct
cerveja, a beer/lager
cervejaria, a large café serving beer and shellfish
chá, o tea
chamada, a call
chamar-se to be called
    chamo-me my name is
chapéu de sol, o parasol
chapéu, o hat
chave, a key
chávena, a cup
chegada, a arrival
chegar to arrive
cheio/a full
cherne, o turbot
chouriço, o spicy red sausage
chumbo, o filling (at dentist's)
churrascaria, a large café specializing in grilled or barbecue food
chuveiro, o shower
cidade, a city/town
cigarro, o cigarette
cinema, o cinema
cinto de salvação, o life-belt, life-ring
cinto, o belt
cinzeiro, o ashtray
cinzento/a grey
claro/a light (-coloured), clear
classe, a class
cobertor, o blanket
cobrar to charge, collect

cofre, o safe-deposit box
cogumelo, o mushroom
colar, o necklace
colher, o spoon
colher de chá, o teaspoon
colherzinha, a teaspoon
collant, o tights
com with
com gás sparkling (mineral water)
com licença excuse me (to get past)
comboio, o train
começar to begin
comer to eat
comerciante de vinhos, o wine merchant's
comida, a food
comissão, a commission
como how/like
como disse? pardon?
carimbar to stamp (ticket)
computador portátil, o laptop
comprar to buy
compreender to understand
comprimidos, os pills, tablets
concerto, o concert
confeitaria, a café for cakes and pastries
conhaque, o cognac
conhecer to know (a person or place)
constipação, a cold
consulta, a appointment (with doctor, dentist)
conta, a bill
conter to contain
contraceptivos, os contraceptives
contrôlo, o control
copo, o glass
cor, a colour
cor-de-laranja orange (colour)
cor-de-rosa pink
correio, o post office, post
correr to run
cortar to cut
cortina, a curtain
costas, as back
cotovelo, o elbow
couro, o leather
couve portuguesa, a kale
couve-flor, a cauliflower
coxa, a thigh
creme para bronzear, o suntan cream
creme, o cream
crer to think
creio I think
criança, a child
cuecas, as underpants
custar to cost

D

daqui a uma hora in one hour
dar to give
de from/of
dedos do pé, os toes
dedos, os fingers
deitar-se to lie down
deixar to leave
demorar to delay
dente, o tooth
dentista, o/a dentist
depois next, later
depois de after
depósito de bagagens, o left-luggage
descafeinado decaffeinated
descansar to rest
descer to get off, go down
desconto, o discount
desculpe excuse me! (to attract attention)/sorry
desejar to desire, want
desodorizante, o deodorant
despir to undress
destino, o destination
desvio, o diversion
detergente para a louça, o washing-up liquid
devagar slowly
dever to have to, must
dia, o day
diabético/a diabetic
diarreia, a diarrhoea
dias úteis, os weekdays
dinheiro, o money
direcção, a steering/address
directo/a direct
direita, a right
discman, o cd player
discoteca, a discotheque
dispa-se get undressed
distracções, as distractions, entertainment
dizer to say, tell
do, da of the (sing)
doce sweet
doer to hurt
dói (it) hurts
doem (they) hurt
dor, a pain
dormida, a room to let
dormir to sleep
dos, das of the (pl)
dose, a portion
duas vezes twice, two times
duche, o shower
durar to last

E

é (it, he, she) is/(you) are
ela her, it/she
ele him, it/he
eléctrico, o tram
elevador, o funicular/lift
em in
  em baixo downstairs
  em cima upstairs
  em frente opposite
embriagem, a clutch
ementa, a menu
encher to fill
encomendar to order
encontrar to find
endereço, o address
enfermeiro/a, o/a nurse
enganar-se to make a mistake
engolir to swallow
entrada, a entrance
entrecosto, o rib
equitação, a horseriding
escada, a stairs
escola, a school
escova de dentes, a toothbrush
escuro/a dark
esgotado/a sold out
espargos, os asparagus
especialidade, a speciality
espectáculo, o show
esperar to wait (for)
espreguiçadeira, a sunlounger
esquerda, a left
esquadra de polícia, a police station
esqui aquático, o waterskiing/waterski
esquina, a corner
estação, a station
estacionamento, o parking
estacionar to park
estádio, o stadium
estalagem, a inn
estar to be (see p134)
este, o east
este/a this
estes/as these
estômago, o stomach
estore, o blind (for window)
estrada, a road
estreito/a narrow
estudante, o/a student
exactamente exactly
examinar to examine
excursão, a excursion, trip
exercício, o exercise
experimentar to try (on)
exposição,a exhibition

F

faca, a knife
falar to speak
família, a family
farinha, a flour
farmácia, a chemist's
faróis, os headlights
fatia, a slice
fato de banho, o swimming costume
fato de treino, o tracksuit
favas, as broad beans
fazer to do, make
febre, a fever
fechado/a closed
fechar to close
feijões verdes green beans
feira, a market/funfair
férias, as holidays
ferro, o iron
ferry-boat, o ferry
festa, a fiesta/celebration/party
fiambre, o ham (boiled)
ficar to be (situated)/remain
ficha, a form
fígado, o liver
figo, o fig
filha, a daughter
filho, o son
filigranas, as filigree jewellery
filme, o film
fim, o end
florista, a florist's
fogos de artifício, os fireworks
fora outside
fósforos, os matches
foto(grafia), a photo(graph), print
fraldas, as nappies
framboesa, a raspberry
frasco, o jar
fresco/a ice cold/cool
frio/a cold
fronha, a pillow case
fumador, o smoker
fumar to smoke
funcionar to work, function
fundo, o back, background
futebol, o football

G

galão, o white coffee (large, milky)
galeria de arte, a art gallery
galo de Barcelos, o the Barcelos cock
gamba, a prawn
garagem, a garage
garfo, o fork
garganta, a throat
garoto, o white coffee (small)
garrafa, a bottle

asóleo, o diesel
asolina, a petrol
elo, o ice
in-tónico, o gin and tonic
inásio, o fitness centre, gym
olfe, o golf
ostar de to like
gosto dele/a I like it, him/her
gosto deles/as I like them
rama, o gramme
rande large
rande armazém, o department store
rãos-de-bico, os chickpeas
rátis free
ravata, a tie
rave serious
rávida pregnant
relhado/a grilled
uarda-sol, o parasol
uardanapo, o napkin
uardar to keep
uia, o guidebook
uiado/a guided

á there is/are
idroplano, o hydrofoil
oje today
omem, o man
ospedaria, a hostel

greja, a church
mperial, a draught beer
mpermeável, o raincoat
mpresso, o form
mprimir to print
ncluído/a included
ncluir to include
nformações, as information
nsecto, o insect
nsolação, a sunstroke
nteressado/a interested
ntervalo, o interval
r to go
sso that (neutral)
sto this (neutral)
VA, o VAT

anela, a window
ardim, o garden
arro, o jug, carafe
oalharia, a jeweller's
oelho, o knee
ogar to play (sport)
ogo, o game, match
óias, as jewellery
ornal, o newspaper

L
lá there
lábios, os lips
ladrão, o/ ladrona, a thief
lamento I'm sorry
lâminas de barbear, as razor blades
lâmpada, a lamp
lápis, o pencil
laranja, a orange (fruit)
laranjada, a orangeade
largo, o square
largo/a wide, broad
lata, a tin, can
lavabos, os toilets
lavandaria (a seco), a laundry (dry cleaner's)
lavatório, o sink
legendas, as subtitles
leitaria, a dairy
leitor de mp3,o mp3 player
leite, o milk
lençóis, os sheets
lenços, os handkerchiefs
lenços de papel, os tissues
lentes de contacto, as contact lenses
lentilhas, as lentils
levantar-se to get up
leve light
libra esterlina, a pound sterling
lição, a lesson
ligação, a connection
ligação exterior, a outside call (telephone)
limão, o lemon
limonada, a lemonade
limpador de pára-brisas, o windscreen wiper
linha, a line, track, platform
líquido, o liquid
lista, a list
livraria, a bookseller's
livre free, available
loção, a lotion
loção hidratante, a moisturiser
loja, a shop
loja de artigos desportivos, a sports shop
loja de artigos fotográficos, a camera shop
loja de brinquedos, a toy shop
loja de ferragens, a hardware store
loja de lembranças, a souvenir shop
loja de produtos dietéticos, a health food shop
loja de roupas, a clothes shop
longe far
louças de barro, as earthenware
louças de porcelana, as china

lugar, o place, site
lula, a squid
luvas, as gloves

M

maçã, a apple
madeira, a wood
maior bigger
mais more
mais alguma coisa? anything else?
mais tarde later
mal passado/a underdone (meat)
mala, a suitcase
mandar to send
mandei reservar I have a reservation
mantenha-se keep, stay
mão, a hand
mapa, o map
máquina fotográfica (digital), a (digital) camera
marcar to dial
mariscos, os shellfish, seafood
marisqueira, a shellfish and seafood restaurant
mastigar to chew
matrícula, a registration number (of car)
medicamento, o medicine
médico/a, o/a doctor
médio/a medium
meia pensão half board
meio/a half
mel, o honey
melancia, a watermelon
melão, o melon
mercado, o market
mercearia, a food shop/grocer's
mesa, a table
mesquita, a mosque
meter to put (in)
metro, o underground/metre
meu, o my
mexer to move
minha, a my
moda, a fashion
molho, o sauce
morar em to live
morada, a address
morango, o strawberry
morder to bite
motocicleta, a motorbike
motor, o engine (of car)
mudar to change
muito very
muito prazer nice to meet you
muito/a/os/as much/many
mulher, a woman
museu, o museum

N

nada nothing
nadar to swim
não no, not
não tem de quê you're welcome
nariz, o nose
natural room temperature
náuseas, as nausea
negócios, os business
no, na in the (singular)
noite, a night
logo then, next
nome, o name
norte, o north
nos, nas in the (plural)
nozes, as walnuts
numerado/a numbered
número, o number, size

O

o, os the (m)
obliterar to punch (ticket)
obras, as roadworks
obrigado/a thank you
oculista, o optician
óculos de sol, os sunglasses
ocupado/a occupied, taken
oeste, o west
olá! hello!
óleo, o oil
olhar to look
olho, o eye
ombro, o shoulder
onde where
ontem yesterday
operação, a operation
orelha, a (outer) ear
osso, o bone
ouvido, o (inner) ear
ovo (estrelado), o (fried) egg

P

pacote, o packet
pacotinho, o sachet
padaria, a bread shop
pãozinho, o bread roll
pagar to pay (for)
palitos, os toothpicks
pão, o bread
papel, o paper
papel higiénico, o toilet paper
papelaria, a stationer's
papo-secos, os bread rolls
para for, towards
paragem, a stop
parar to stop
parque, o park
parque de campismo, o campsite

arque de estacionamento, o car park
artida, a departure
artido/a broken
artir to depart
assadeira (de calças), a trouser press
assaporte, o passport
asta, a briefcase
asta de dentes, a toothpaste
astéis de Belém/nata, os custard tarts
astelaria, a café or shop for cakes
 and pastries
atins, os rollerblades/skates
az, a peace
é, o foot
eagem, a toll
eça, a part (of car)
edir to order, ask for
eixaria, a fishmonger's
eixe, o fish
ele, a leather/skin
ensão, a guesthouse
ensão completa, a full board
ensar to think
ensos higiénicos, os sanitary towels
ente, o comb
eões, os pedestrians
equeno/a small
equeno almoço, o breakfast
êra, a pear
erder to lose
erdidos e achados lost property
erigo, o danger
ermitido allowed
erna, a leg
erto near
erto daqui near here
escoço, o neck
êssego, o peach
essoa, a person
etiscos, os titbits, snacks
eúgas, as socks
icada, a sting
icar to sting
ilha, a battery
imenta, a pepper (seasoning)
imento, o pepper (vegetable)
ires, o saucer
iripiri, o chilli and olive oil seasoning
iscina, a swimming pool
istacho, o pistachio
lanta, a map, plan (of town)
lateia, a stalls (in theatre)
neu, o tyre
neu furado, o flat tyre
oder to be able, can
olícia, a police
onte, a bridge

por for/by/per/along
  por quanto tempo for how long
por favor please
porta, a door, gate
portagem, a toll
portão, o gate
porto, o port
português/esa Portuguese
posso I can
postal, o postcard
posto de turismo, o Tourist Office
pousada, a up-market hotel
pousada de juventude, a youth hostel
praça, a square, market
praça de táxis, a taxi rank
praia, a beach
prancha à vela, a windsurf board
prancha de surf, a surfboard
prancha de wind-surf, a windsurf board
prato, o plate, dish/course
pré-pagamento, o payment in advance
preço, o price
preencher to fill in
prego, o steak sandwich
presunto, o ham (smoked)
preto/a black
primeiro/a first
prioridade, a priority
prisão de ventre, a constipation
problema, o problem
programa, o programme
proibido forbidden
pronto ready
provador, o fitting room
provar to try (on)
provisório/a temporary
próximo/a next
pulôver, o pullover
pulso, o wrist
púrpura purple
puxador, o handle

Q

quando when
quanto how much
quarto, o room/quarter
  quarto duplo, o double room
  quarto individual, o single room
que what
  que horas são? what time is it?
queijada, a cheesecake/cheese tart
queijo, o cheese
queimadura, a burn
queimadura solar, a sunburn
queimar to burn
queixo, o chin
quem who, whom

quente hot
querer to wish, want
queria I'd like
quilo, o kilo
quilómetro, o kilometre
quiosque de jornais, o news-stand

R

radiador, o radiator
rádio, o radio
rapaz, o boy
rapariga, a girl
raqueta, a racket
rebuçados, os sweets
receita, a prescription
recheado/a stuffed
recibo, o receipt
recomendar to recommend
reduzir to reduce
refeição, a meal
reformado/a retired
refrigerante, o soft drink
região, a region
regressar to return
relógio, o watch
rendas, as lacework
repetir to repeat
rés-do-chão, o ground floor
reservado/a reserved
reservar to reserve
residencial, o hotel
restaurante, o restaurant
retrete, o toilet
revelar to develop (film)
revista, a magazine
rins, os kidneys
rissóis, os fried pasties
roda, a wheel
rolo, o roll (of film)
roubar to steal, rob
roupa, a clothes
rua, a street

S

saber to know
sabonete, o soap
sabor, o flavour
saco, o bag
saco de mão, o handbag
saia, a skirt
saída, a exit
sal, o salt
sala de concertos, a concert hall
sala de espera, a waiting room
sala de reunião, a meeting room
salada, a salad
salão de chá, o tea room
salsa, a parsley
salva-vidas, o/a lifeguard

sandálias, as sandals
sanitários, os toilets
são (they, you) are
sapataria, a shoe shop
sapatos, os shoes
sardinhas, as sardines
saúde, a health
sauna, a sauna
se faz favor please
secador de cabelo, o hairdryer
secção, a section, department
seco/a dry
segundo/a second
segurança, a security
seguro, o insurance
sei I know
selo, o stamp
sem without
  sem chumbo unleaded
  sem gás still (mineral water)
  sem saída no through road
semana, a week
sempre always
sempre em frente straight on
senhor, o you (m, very formal)/man,
  gentleman
senhora, a you (f, very formal)/woman,
  lady
sentar-se to sit down
sentido proibido no access
sentir-se to feel
ser to be (see p134)
serviço, o service
seu, o your/his/its (m)
seus, os their(s) (m)
sim yes
simples single/simple
sinal, o deposit/signal
só only
sobremesa, a pudding, dessert
socorro! help!
sofrer to suffer
solteiro/a single, not married
sou I am
soutien, o bra
sua, a your/hers/its (f)
suas, as their(s) (f)
sujo/a dirty
sujar to make something dirty
sul, o south
sumo de fruta, o fruit juice
super, o four-star (petrol)
supermercado, o supermarket
suplemento, o supplement
surf, o surfing

abacaria, a tobacconist's
acos de golfe, os golf clubs
alho, o butcher's
âmaras, as dates
anto faz it doesn't matter
apete, o rug
arde late
arde, a afternoon/evening
asca, a tavern
eatro, o theatre
elefone, o telephone
elemóvel, o mobile phone
elevisão, a television
em (you) have/(he/she/it) has
emos (we) have
emplo, o temple
enda, a tent
enho I have
énis, o tennis
er to have
erminar to end, finish
erraço, o terrace
esta, a forehead
igela, a bowl
ipo, o type
irar to pull out, take out
  tirar fotografias to take photos
oalha, a towel
oalha de mesa, a tablecloth
oalhas absorventes, as sanitary
  towels
omada, a plug (socket)
omar to take, have
omate, o tomato
oranja, a grapefruit
orneira, a tap
ornozelo, o ankle
orrada, a piece of toast
osse, a cough
osta, a toasted sandwich
  tosta mista, a toasted cheese and
  ham sandwich
ourada, a bullfight
rabalhar to work
ravões, os brakes
razer to bring
rocar to change
roco, o change
udo all, everything

U

ísque, o whisky
um pouco a little (i.e. not much)
uma vez once, one time
unhas, as nails
uns, umas some
urgente urgent

usar to use
uvas, as grapes

V

vagens, as green beans
vago/a free, unoccupied
vai (he, she) goes/(you) go
varanda, a balcony
vários/as several
vegetariano/a vegetarian
vela, a sailing/sail
velocidade, a speed
ver to see
verde green
vermelho/a red
vestiário, o cloakroom
vestido, o dress
vila, a town
vinagre, o vinegar
vinho, o wine
  vinho do Porto, o port
virar to turn
visita, a visit
vista, a view
viúva, a widow
viúvo, o widower
você you (fairly polite, see p132)
volante, o steering wheel
voleibol, o volleyball
voltar to return
vomitar to vomit
voo, o flight
vou I go, am going

W

wind-surf, o windsurfing

X

xaile, o shawl
xarope para a tosse, o cough mixture

Z

zona, a zone, area
zona comercial, a shopping area